CONFLICT
Resolution
for
Law Enforcement

Street-Smart Negotiating

Kyle E. Blanchfield
Thomas A. Blanchfield
Peter D. Ladd

43-08 162nd Street
Flushing, NY 11358
www.LooseleafLaw.com
800-647-5547

This publication is not intended to replace nor be a substitute for any official procedural material issued by your agency of employment nor other official source. Looseleaf Law Publications, Inc., the author and any associated advisors have made all possible efforts to ensure the accuracy and thoroughness of the information provided herein but accept no liability whatsoever for injury, legal action or other adverse results following the application or adoption of the information contained in this book.

Library of Congress In-Publication Data

Blanchfield, Kyle E.
  Conflict resolution for law enforcement : street-smart negotiating / Kyle E. Blanchfield, Thomas A. Blanchfield, Peter D. Ladd.
      p. cm.
  Includes bibliographical references and index.
  ISBN 978-1-932777-44-4
  1. Police training--United States. 2. Law enforcement--United States. 3. Conflict management--United States. 4. Mediation--United States. I. Blanchfield, Thomas A. II. Ladd, Peter D. III. Title.
  HV8142.B53 2008
  363.2'3--dc22

                                                              2007041351

1st Printing - 2008
2nd Printing - 2009
3rd Printing - 2010

Cover design by: *Sans Serif, Inc.*, Saline, Michigan

Dedication

Dedicated to law enforcement officers,
who risk their lives
to protect citizens and their communities.

Table of Contents

Part II Mediation Training

Chapter 10

PREFACE

I n the law enforcement training academies across the United States, a need exists for a comprehensive understanding of mediation and conciliation skills and how these skills apply to the profession of law enforcement. For example, research shows that only around 30% of calls responded to by law enforcement officers end in an arrest. The professional question is, "What happens to the other 70% of the calls?" For the most part, these calls are left open-ended, where the dispute causing law enforcement assistance goes unanswered; it does not rise to the level of an arrest. Unfortunately, experience shows that without some form of closure to these disputes, the rate of recidivism will remain high. Many disputes not rising to the level of an arrest can build over time, causing repeated calls to law enforcement agencies.

The book that we have written takes into account the reality of law enforcement officers who have to face disputes on a daily basis. It guides the reader through 9 of the most common disputes facing law enforcement and discusses solutions based on what a law enforcement officer's responsibility is under the law. However, the book goes beyond the 30% of calls ending in an arrest. Mediation and conciliation skills are applied to the same 9 disputes facing law enforcement with an ongoing review from one chapter to another, ending in a comprehensive mediation training program as a final review in Chapter 10. Our purpose is to develop an understanding of how to mediate or conciliate the 70% of law enforcement calls that do not end in an arrest.

Our goal is to supply law enforcement with a practical, straightforward book that focuses on mediation and conciliation skills for law enforcement officers. Our approach of describing legal remedies as compared to mediation or conciliation remedies to everyday disputes, we believe, will strengthen the professional skills of the law enforcement community.

We would like to thank those law enforcement officers who generously advised us in making this book possible. We are indebted to the people who shared their experiences with us as they related time-tested solutions to complex problems. We relied on the observations and suggestions of veteran administrators, those who were "in the trenches":

Chief Gregg DeLuca, Little Falls, NY and former Under Sheriff of Herkimer County provided training manuals from DCJS, (Division of Criminal Justice Services) as a guide to the process in training academies in NY State. His unbridled passion for police training, both basic and supervisory, included pro-active suggestions for initiating training standards and was an inspiration to the authors as he reviewed our concepts and encouraged us in the need for dispute resolution as an alternative. His 36 years of being "on the street" were invaluable and professionally informative in our pursuit for accurate and recognizable information.

Chief Raymond Philo, New Hartford, NY has our gratitude as he helped to direct our effort by referring to the many field situations and confrontations that could employ mediation and conciliation. He had a positive and encouraging effect on our writings as he reviewed the multitude of calls that could be defused through the efforts of the police officer, using mediation as a diversion to arrest. His 26 years in law enforcement has produced an appreciation for alternatives.

The insight and sharing, the day-to-day calls and crises that could be resolved through the mediation process, was extremely helpful as we interviewed Officer Seth Cresswell, Kirkland P.D., NY. He was a positive and encouraging source as he referenced through memory actions that could have allayed by the mediation means.

NYSP retired Trooper, Robert Wolkowski, reinforced the notion that mediation can and has worked as he spent his valuable time supporting our endeavor to produce a qualitative manual as a training aid and device for basic and supervisory personnel.

SUNY (State University of New York) University Police Lieutenant Merritt Hunt, SUNY, Oneonta, relayed the importance of mediation as a vital option as he dealt with college students over the past 28 years. He selected many cases that could have been appropriate for a mutual conclusion other than arrest.

Patrick Trophia, supervisor, Oneida County, NY, Probation Department for 28 years was an interviewee who was a strong contributor for after the fact determinations. It was his balance for cases that he supervised that was "post adjudication" as he second-guessed the system that he revered and considered the action taken as the wrong avenue, and that mediation would have, and could have been used in a more timely and effective manner.

The urban scenarios were the product of many memories shared by Michael Dapuzzo, former Federal Police Officer, US Department of Defense, SWAT Team Member. We are thankful for the time and interest he displayed as he recounted case after case of real situations that could have been resolved if mediation was applied, both for the defendant and the arresting agency.

Also, we would like to thank Louie Mitchell, Chief of Police for the Akwesasne Mohawk Nation. His insights of how to face domestic confrontations were invaluable for completing our research.

It became apparent during our interviews as we attempted to balance the theoretical with the reality of police work that the viability of mediation was almost exclusively restricted to the mind set of the veteran officers and administrators, and that newly trained police officers felt that the option was less acceptable in response to their mission and that arrest was the primary option to response.

Finally, we would like to acknowledge those professionals in law enforcement who risk their lives every day in the service of the general public. We hope this book will better serve them when an arrest may not be the most productive way of solving a problem. We believe that law enforcement officers do not have to be expert mediators and conciliators in order to make a difference. Simply, having an understanding and desire to use the skills found in this book may make a dramatic change in people's behavior. In that regard, we dedicate this book to those public servants who keep us safe and protected.

Kyle E. Blanchfield JD
Thomas A. Blanchfield, MA, Professor Emeritus
Peter D. Ladd PhD

Part I

Conflict Resolution for Law Enforcement

Chapter 1

HARASSMENT

Introduction

The term harassment in law enforcement can take in many different meanings. There is sexual harassment found in the workplace where the most common scenario is when a dominant employer is harassing a subservient employee. In these cases, the harassment can be verbal, physical, sexual, or all three and many harassment cases have filled our courts in the last thirty years, where one person is dominant over another (Achambong, 1999). Most of these fall under charges of sexual discrimination under Title VII of the Civil Rights Act of 1964 and its 1972 amendments and the Equal Protections Clause of the 14th Amendment (Lenhart, 2004), and many are civil actions based on common law, such as negligence, infliction of emotional distress, interference with contractual relationships and wrongful discharge (Shultz, 1998).

However, in the everyday practice of law enforcement, other examples come to mind that may have a more criminal disposition. One of the most common calls law enforcement officers make, centers around some form of harassment, especially in domestic disputes and most of these disputes can be highly emotional where just knowing the law may not be enough to resolve the problem (Ray, 2001). These are disputes where one party is trying to get dominance over the other; physically, emotionally and possibly sexually. The response to such a call can have legal as well as conflict resolution solutions connected to it. Many times, the decision to arrest someone or try to resolve the dispute between the parties is a judgment call that must be made quickly. Here is an overview of the law on harassment that should be considered when responding to a harassment call.

Legal Criteria and Harassment

Harassment complaints take in several variables when considering an effective response by law enforcement officers. In this section we will consider some of those variables and look at numerous

3

criteria that may or may not change an officer's thinking when responding to a harassment complaint. The following represents basic criteria to consider when responding to a complaint of harassment:

1st Degree Harassment

The major point to make when considering 1st degree harassment cases can be summed up in the following statement extracted from New York State Penal Code, Section 240.25 which states that 1st degree harassment can be determined by, "repeatedly committing acts which places people in reasonable fear of physical injury." This definition brings a few key points for law enforcement officers to consider in responding to harassment cases:

Repeatedly Committing Acts — It may be important for law enforcement officers to differentiate between an isolated event of harassment and a continual pattern where harassment is used against another person or persons. Isolated events of harassment do not necessarily show any intent or plan to harass another and as first time offenses could be handled as a class B misdemeanor with possible probation and a conditional discharge. However, repeatedly committing acts of harassment may direct the law enforcement officer to consider a chronic problem that may persist after the officer has responded to the call. Harassment, as a one-time event, may indicate that the situation has gotten out of control and has turned into a dispute where people have gone from reasonable methods of solving their disputes to methods that include: threatening, challenging, shouting and other forms of harassing behavior. On the other hand, repeatedly committing acts of harassment may indicate an *intentional plan* to harass, which may go beyond a dispute being out of control and indicate some intentional plan for revenge by harassing another person or persons. Law enforcement officers responding to a harassment call may want to consider whether the harassment complaint is a dispute that has become out of control or is it based on an intentional plan to repeatedly commit acts of harassment.

Reasonable Fear of Physical Injury — In establishing a 1st degree harassment in New York State the ideas of physical injury increases, with the harasser repeatedly committing acts of harassment. People who continually harass have a tendency to escalate their harassment especially if the prior harassment did not achieve its intended effect on the victim. This pattern of harassment may end in some form of physical injury, especially if it is premeditated and planned. At some point, the law enforcement officer must determine whether the harassment case will eventually end in an act of assault.

Aggravated Harassment — A law enforcement officer must also consider prior convictions in order to respond to a harassment complaint effectively. If it is determined that a person has a 1st or 2nd degree harassment charge in the last ten years then that may dramatically change the officer's thinking. Under these circumstances the harasser has met the letter of the Law on two points:

1. He has repeatedly committed acts of harassment and has been convicted at least twice and,
2. He has established the possibility of there being fear of physical injury in having at least two harassment convictions. At this point, the harasser could be charged with aggravated harassment; the term *aggravated* makes harassment a more serious matter.*

It means that the harasser probably intends to go beyond just harassment. Harassment may become a starting point for more serious offenses such as physical abuse, assault and even murder. In responding to harassment, officers may need to consider the criteria necessary for establishing whether: Is this complaint a *repeatedly committed act?* Does it rise to the level of *reasonable fear of physical injury?* And, has it reached the level of *aggravated harassment?* (Aggravated Harassment, 2nd degree, NYS Penal Law, Section 240.30)

---

*When *aggravated* appears as a higher level of criminality, it means **"worsen-upgrade."** Webster's Dictionary definition is, "In legal terms some feature that makes the crime more serious, brings to a higher level." e.g. simple assault is without a weapon, aggravated assault is with a weapon. A predicated crime becomes an aggravated crime and the sanction is increased. (Webster, 1992)

2nd Degree Harassment

The major point when considering 2nd degree harassment can be summed up from the following statement extracted from New York State Penal Law, Section (240.26) which states that 2nd degree harassment can be determined by, "acts which alarm or seriously annoy such other person, which serve no legitimate purpose." Again, this definition brings a few key points for law enforcement officers to consider in responding to harassment cases:

Alarm and Seriously Annoying Others — In 2nd degree harassment cases the focus of the complaint shifts. For example, "Is the harasser **seriously annoying others?**" In 2nd degree harassment cases it is others who become the focus. The law enforcement officer must consider both the harasser's behavior but also its effect on others. If he or she determines that the harasser is alarming and annoying others but is not repeatedly committing acts that cause reasonable fear of injury, then the officer's thinking may begin to shift to considering a 2nd degree charge of harassment. The importance for the law enforcement officer is that a 2nd degree charge of harassment is not a misdemeanor; it is a violation, not a crime. Alarming and seriously annoying others can be a violation of a relationship with others and is treated as a violation under the law. In this case, the harasser may end up with an appearance ticket before a judge for annoying behavior but he has not established the criteria needed to be classified as a criminal.

Behavior Serving No Legitimate Purpose — Law enforcement officers also may want to consider whether the harasser's alarming and annoying behavior serves any legitimate purpose. In other words, "What purpose does it serve to be alarming and annoying the neighborhood at 2 o'clock in the morning?" Here is where the law enforcement officer may want to consider the harasser's intentions. It must be pointed out that in harassment cases the purpose of people's behavior is to harass, not to resolve a dispute. Again, if the law enforcement officer discovers that the harasser's behavior has no purpose but to harass others, then he may want to consider a 2nd degree harassment charge. Also, the law enforcement officer probably may want to consider a section of the penal law in their state. For example, the New York State Penal Law Section (Title N, Article

240) and realizes that the harasser could create a situation where the harassment complaint becomes a catalyst for other violations or crimes such as: riot, stalking, unlawful assembly, sexual abuse and disorderly conduct. Here we see where "behavior serving no legitimate purpose" can cause an escalating conflict for the community.

Case Study

The problems between Tom and Lisa were not new to the local law enforcement officers. Since their divorce the police had responded to numerous calls where either Tom or Lisa wanted the other arrested for harassment. The fact that they lived in the same neighborhood did not make matters any easier, and that their two children were constantly caught in the middle of their offensive behavior made an effective form of conflict resolution an immediate concern. Especially, since both children were now being reported for bullying others in school.

Delaney was one of the law enforcement officers who understood this couple better than most. He had, on numerous occasions, responded to calls where one of them was calling at inappropriate times of the night, yelling at the other in front of the neighbors, threatening to disrupt their newly-found relationships and even an occasional heavy breathing on the phone and then hanging up. To make matters worse, he also knew that the harassing behavior was escalating. It not only was affecting the behavior of their children but it was causing social problems in their community. Neighbors were beginning to ask, "What are our local law enforcement officers going to do about this problem? Why don't they arrest somebody?"

It seemed to Officer Delaney and other law enforcement officers that making an arrest was certainly a viable option, yet other options were available, and threatening them with an arrest had not, till this point, curtailed their behavior. It was under these circumstances that Officer Delaney was asked to respond to a call at 2 o'clock in the morning from Lisa's residence. Apparently, Tom was at the front door banging on it and forcefully screaming that she was a terrible mother and how the entire neighborhood should know how rotten she had been over the years.

Since Delaney was involved with the complaint before, he quickly thought of aggravated harassment being an option, if Tom

was convicted during the last 10 years for 1st and 2nd degree harassment. He hoped it would not reach that level; a second degree for a
repeat offender is an A misdemeanor. He, also, hoped it did not
reach a 1st degree harassment charge; that could translate into an E
felony. As he was driving, other words came to his mind such as,
order of protection and *trespass*. He started to think about the Penal
Law, especially the section that dealt with public order. The terms:
riot, stalking, unlawful assembly, sexual abuse, loitering, disorderly
conduct and harassment came to mind (New York State Penal Law,
Section 240.20)

When Delaney arrived at Lisa's house he kept two options open
in his mind. The first was, "What needed to happen in order to
warrant an arrest for harassment?" The second option was, "How
could he reconcile this dispute so that everyone calmed down
without an arrest being warranted?" The following criteria should
be considered when responding to this and other harassment
disputes:

Conflict Resolution and Harassment

In reviewing the legal criteria to consider when responding to
harassment, it may become apparent that numerous other variables
are affected when considering a harassment complaint. To a certain
degree, complaints rising to the level of 1st degree harassment are
more likely to be settled legally, especially aggravated harassment
complaints (Blanchfield & Lenahan, 2004). However, when a law
enforcement officer responds to a harassment complaint that only
rises to the level of 2nd degree harassment, we have seen that the
focus can shift away from the harasser and refocus on the alarm and
annoyance of others. Under these circumstances, conflict resolution
skills may benefit not only the harassing party but also all of those
individuals caught within the harassment. The following are conflict
resolution skills to consider when responding to harassment complaints that do not rise to the level of a violation or a crime:

Finding Common Ground—What Officer Delaney may want to
consider in approaching Tom and Lisa is that the harassment may
have become so alarming and annoying that whatever common
ground they had between them has been lost. Tom and Lisa may feel
polarized or "far apart" on many issues that they once had in

common. If Officer Delaney can reestablish common ground between them, there may be little need to continue any form of harassing behavior. Let us look at some common ground that Officer Delaney may use to reconcile this complaint:

Can they both agree:

- They love their children?
- There are other ways to solve their problems?
- Harassment can create fear in others?
- Their children are becoming bullies?
- Their problems should not be shared with the neighbors?
- At the present time they do not like each other?

Harassment is partially defined as alarming and annoying behavior serving no legitimate purpose. Establishing common ground through any of the above statements may begin to bring Lisa and Tom together for a common purpose. Even the common ground that, "they agree not to like each other" is an agreement with a purpose. If they do not like each other that does not mean they cannot consider the needs of their children, the neighbors or even their personal fears. If nothing else, establishing common ground may have a dramatic affect on reducing a fear of physical injury (Barsky, 2000).

Reframing Annoying and Alarming Language — Officer Delaney may be able to reconcile the harassment complaint by getting Tom to reframe the way he is talking to Lisa. Harassment is caused by language that is not considered reasonable or acceptable and it is usually language judged as having no purpose, except to annoy and alarm. Reconciling this may take on a number of forms (Ladd, 2005):

- *Tone of Voice* – He may ask Tom to lower his tone of voice and speak more slowly. He may also ask Lisa to do the same. By lowering the tone of voice and slowing down the pace of the conversation, Officer Delaney may be able to re-introduce reasonable dialogue to resolve the dispute.

- *Freeze Words* – People who harass others often use language filled with epithets, slander, insults, slurs and defamatory statements. Officer Delaney may want to convince both Tom and Lisa to remove these words from their dispute. Usually when people use any of the above language, the receiver of this language has a tendency to freeze on those words causing them the most alarm and annoyance. Many harassment complaints start with such words and their main purpose is to create alarm, annoyance and sometimes fear. Removing these words can help a Law Enforcement Officer get to the core of the disputes.

Caucusing—In harassment cases it may be important for the law enforcement officers to practice some form of "shuttle diplomacy," usually referred to as caucusing. This is where the two parties are separated in order to hear both sides of the complaint. In the case study Officer Delaney could have Lisa wait in another room while he talks to Tom. He then may take valuable information from their discussion and share it with Lisa in a separate discussion. In the case of Officer Delaney, he now may be in a position to share pieces of information that have a purpose, without the alarming language, with the hope of reducing people's fears and in the hope of establishing significant common ground. However, there are two other benefits from caucusing (Blanchfield & Ladd, 1989):

- *Spatial Distance* – By separating Tom and Lisa, Officer Delaney has a better chance of both parties calming down and becoming more reasonable. He has also reduced the chances of the harassment complaint escalating in possible assault and other forms of physical abuse. Spatial distance gives both parties a chance to reconsider their actions and behavior.

- *Temporal Distance* – After using spatial distance at 2 o'clock in the morning to separate Tom and Lisa, Officer Delaney might decide that checking back the next day and having both sides reconsider the actions of the night before, may be an attempt at curtailing the harassment. Many cases similar to harassment cases have a high recidivism rate because the law enforcement officer failed to obtain closure.

Establishing Boundaries—Part of the reality in responding to a harassment complaint is that harassment steps over the boundaries of what is reasonable and purposeful (Gladding, 2002). This can be seen in the legal definition of 2nd degree harassment. Harassment is alarming and seriously annoying behavior that serves no legitimate purpose (New York State Penal Law, Section 240.26). Harassment has a way of knocking down the boundaries between what is reasonable and unreasonable. In the case study, Officer Delaney has an opportunity to reestablish these boundaries and have both parties agree to them. For example, he can establish the following boundaries:

- Let us agree on a reasonable time to visit each other at night.

- Let us agree on the type of language we will use in front of the children.

- Let us agree that our arguments have a purpose and are not only to harass the other party.

- Let us agree on how we are going to act in front of the neighbors.

- Let us agree on what other measures we need to take if our communication breaks down.

- Let us agree that we will not try to solve problems while we are drinking.

Creating boundaries in any one of these areas could have a dramatic effect on the outcome of the harassment complaint and could dramatically impact repeated calls to law enforcement about this complaint.

Victim Offender Mediation—Another alternative open to Officer Delaney, may take place after the alarming and annoying behavior has stopped and the fear of physical injury has passed. Harassment cases are not the type of complaints that law enforcement officers want to respond to, especially if they are connected to the same parties in the complaint. However, harassment is a type of complaint with a high recidivism rate, when emotional scars from numerous everyday complaints, leaves both sides of the dispute distant and psychologically traumatized. In such circumstance, the victim has an opportunity to face the harassing party through Victim Offender Mediation. There are numerous Restorative Justice Programs across the entire country encouraging the victims of harassment to participate in a Victim Offender Mediation. There is an opportunity for the offender to speak in language that is meaningful and conciliatory, and there is an opportunity for the victim to vent the emotional trauma created by the offender's harassment. However, in order for these mediations to work, both parties have to be of good will — with a true sense of wanting reconciliation (Umbriet, 1997). Officer Delaney may eventually find that Tom and Lisa are now not a common occurrence on the dispatcher's list because they have resolved their disputes by using conflict resolution skills and they have reconciled their disputes through Victim Offender Mediation. This leaves Officer Delaney open to respond to complaints where conflict resolution is not a viable option.

Exercises

Responding to the Case Study (How would Officer Delaney respond to this harassment call from a *legal point of view?*)

Responding to the Case Study (How would Officer Delaney respond to this harassment call from a *conflict resolution point of view?*)

How many options does Officer Delaney have from a legal point of view?

If selecting a conflict resolution stance to the harassment call, Officer Delaney could use what skills?

How can Victim Offender Mediation reduce recidivism in
harassment complaints?

How could finding common ground be useful in harassment
cases?

What could be the benefit of reframing harassing language?

When is an appropriate time to caucus?

Chapter 2

PHYSICAL THREATS: MENACING BEHAVIOR

Introduction

P hysical threats and menacing behavior have taken on new meaning since the tragedy of September 11th, 2001. Since that time, the world has become more vigilant regarding what people say to each other and what they are doing in the presence of each other (Thackrah, 2004). We are living in a dangerous world that increases the vigilance of law enforcement officers on a global scale, and within our rural and urban communities. When we realize that 75% of the large cities in the United States have some form of curfew for its citizens, we begin to understand problems facing law enforcement with those who physically threaten and practice menacing behavior in the presence of strangers, neighbors, families and friends (Werdegar, 1999).

The question may arise as to why one person would threaten another? Some researchers describe it as a way of testing what another person is "made of" (Cohen & Vandello, 1998). While others believe that threatening others is about control and wanting to be the dominant figure in any given dispute (Chamberlain, Eddy & Whaley, 2004). We can see both of these reasons acted out when domestic violence looms in the background of a relationship or when gangs of males have congregated on a street corner with criminal intentions at the base of their activity (Miller, 1997).

Also, closely related to physical threats is menacing behavior that creates a threat to all those who witness the possible beginning stage in future violent behavior. The anxiety and terror that menacing behavior can produce has increased in our dangerous, violent world. The following is an overview of laws on physical threats and menacing behavior that should be considered when responding to a call where one of these two elements is involved:

Legal Criteria and Physical Threats and Menacing Behavior

Physical threats and menacing behavior complaints combine different sections of many State Penal Codes when considering a response by law enforcement officers. In this section, we will consider some of those variables and look at numerous criteria that may or may not change an officer's thinking when responding to physical threats or menacing behavior complaint. The following represents basic criteria to consider when responding to these complaints:

Menacing in the 1st Degree

The major point to make when considering menacing in the 1st degree can be summed up in the following statement extracted from the New York State Penal Law, Section (120.13) which states that menacing in the 1st degree can be determined by, "A person is guilty of menacing in the first degree when he or she commits the crime of menacing in the second degree and has been previously convicted of a crime of menacing within the preceding ten years. In other states, a similar position is taken yet is described in different terms. In California, menacing in the first degree is called willfully threatening to commit a crime, California Penal Code, Section 422–422.1 However, the intent is to demonstrate behavior that has been repeated over time.

Convicted of Previous Physical Threats—In menacing behavior cases, any physical threat should not be tolerated under the law; especially, cases where the perpetrator has been convicted of previous acts of menacing behavior that shows a potential pattern for future behavior. In cases of repeated acts of menacing behavior, the law enforcement officer has a responsibility to protect the rights of those people being violated and has very limited flexibility in trying to resolve disputes outside of making an arrest. In some States, those individuals that have been convicted of repeated acts of menacing behavior should be arrested and charged with a class E felony.

Menacing in the 2nd Degree

The major points to make when considering menacing in the 2nd degree can be understood from the following three points extracted from New York State Penal Law (120.14) which states how menacing in the 2nd degree is determined: He or she intentionally places or attempts to place another person in reasonable fear of physical injury, serious physical injury or death by displaying a deadly weapon or dangerous instrument. Also, menacing behavior in the 2nd degree may tie into some State's Family Court Act as in New York State under section 530.12.where law enforcement officers may consider someone breaking an order of protection issued by the court and its implication when responding to physical threats and menacing behavior cases.

Menacing in the 3rd Degree

A person is guilty of menacing in the 3rd degree when, by physical menace, he or she intentionally places or attempts to place another person in fear of death, imminent serious physical injury or physical injury NYS Penal Code (120.15). Being charged with menacing in the 3rd degree can be considered a class B misdemeanor in some States.

Fear of Physical Injury — Law enforcement officers face a dilemma when considering menacing in the 3rd Degree. In order to arrest someone on a 3rd degree menacing charge the officer cannot rely on a prior conviction in the last ten years. Also, the person will not be holding a pistol or brandishing any other deadly weapon. Most likely, the person or persons will be manifesting high levels of emotion but with imminent threat to someone's life. At this point, it becomes more difficult for a law enforcement officer to decide whether to arrest someone or if there are methods that will effectively end the dispute taking place.

Under these circumstances, it is possible to charge someone with a menacing in the 3rd degree. However, the officer must decide whether such a charge will deter against future threats and menacing behavior. If the officer decides such an arrest will not act as a deterrent, then conflict resolution skills may to be considered in resolving the dispute. The following case study gives you an opportunity to decide this issue:

Case Study

Officer Thomas was considered a highly competent law enforcement officer who went beyond just arresting people when on a call for physical threats and menacing behavior. She knew that recidivism, in such cases, was high and that each return call seemed to place the victim in greater fear of physical injury, with greater possibility for the use of deadly weapons such as: firearms or objects used to inflict harm. She had a reputation for knowing how to resolve disputes between couples and this, combined with her knowledge of the law, made her a professional who was called on when a physical threat complaint was issued to the police dispatcher.

Harriet and George had a history of fighting with each other, especially over how to raise the children. Harriet had custody of Jim, eight years old and Martha, ten years old and George's visitation rights seemed limited, according to George, especially when the children got in trouble in the neighborhood or in school. It was during these periods of time that George would show up at Martha's house, where he would threaten her with some form of physical harm.

Officer Thomas received a call from the dispatcher, that a complaint for possible domestic violence was about to take place. The dispatcher conveyed to Officer Thomas that Martha had given her address and that she and George had a heated exchange on the phone and that he threatened her with bodily harm and was coming over to her house.

Immediately, Officer Thomas went to her patrol car computer to see if any previous violations between them had taken place. She knew that menacing another person in the 1st degree can be a class E felony, if there was a previous conviction for intentionally putting another person in fear of physical injury within the past ten years. She also hoped that no deadly weapons would be involved that warranted menacing in the 2nd degree or that George had not practiced repeated acts of menacing behavior, that was also a 2nd degree menacing charge, because she knew that menacing in the 2nd degree held a charge of a class A misdemeanor. Another consideration that Officer Thomas had to make is whether an Order of Protection was issued according to the Family Court Act, section 530.12 where George was knowledgeable that he should stay away from Martha.

Finally, Officer Thomas had to consider what she would do if George had not used physical violence and was not under an order of protection but was threatening Martha, that could lead to imminent serious physical injury. She knew this behavior warranted menacing in the third degree and was considered a class B misdemeanor.

When Officer Thomas arrived at Martha's house she went through the checklist in her mind:

☐ "Has this incident happened before, and was there a crime committed?"
☐ "Are there any weapons involved?"
☐ "Has an order of protection been filed?"
☐ "Is this individual menacing to the degree that physical bodily harm is imminent?"
☐ "Can this dispute be resolved without an arrest being made?"

The following criteria may be important to consider when responding to this and other domestic violence-oriented cases where menacing behavior needs the expertise of a law enforcement officer who understands the law regarding menacing behavior and orders of protection, and has conflict resolution skills that may prevent physical threats from happening in the first place.

Conflict Resolution and Physical Threats and Menacing Behavior

In reviewing the legal criteria to consider when responding to physical threats and menacing behavior, it may be important to understand that the officer, in these types of complaints, is not responding to a complaint where an assault has been committed. The officer is responding to the threat of physical assault or menacing behavior. In spite of this, menacing behavior through the use of physical threats can hold a class E felony charge, especially if the officer is dealing with someone who has been convicted of the charge at a previous date. In these cases, complaints rising to the level of menacing behavior in the 1st degree are usually settled legally. However, when the law enforcement officer responds to menacing behavior in the 2nd degree and especially menacing behavior in the 3rd degree, the law enforcement officer should be aware of other choices. Under these circumstances, there may be outside issues that are connected to the physical threats or menacing behavior that have a dramatic influence on the resolution of the dispute. It cannot be assumed that in all of these cases an arrest will stop the problems emanating from these couples. In some of these cases conflict resolution skills may be a viable alternative to court action that may deter the couple from future physical threats and menacing behavior.

The Importance of Understanding a Climate of Anger — Anger can be a major factor in many domestic disputes and it may be important to review the stages of anger, in order to grasp the importance of dealing with this emotion through the use of conflict resolution. Anger begins when someone finds the other party's behavior has become unreasonable. In the case study, George did not find Martha's phone conversation reasonable regarding their children. Martha called the police after he slammed the phone down and threatened her by coming over to her house because she felt his behavior was unreasonable. Anger begins with **unreasonable behavior** followed by someone becoming **stressed** and eventually **exploding**. For law enforcement officers the next two stages in resolving anger are crucial, namely: people **need distance** for **reason to return** (Blanchfield K. & Ladd P.,1989) .

- **Spatial Distance** – It becomes difficult to resolve any dispute when people are exploding with anger; people have become unreasonable, they are showing stress and are exploding in some way. Not the best conditions for solving problems that need reasonable resolutions. In the case study, Officer Thomas may need to separate George and Martha in order to get distance for the threatening and menacing behavior to calm down.

- **Temporal Distance** – She may also need time for their threatening and menacing behavior not to interfere with a law enforcement officer's attempts at resolving a dispute where fear of physical threats and menacing behavior are present. In the case study, Officer Thomas may want to take her time and not try to resolve the dispute between them immediately. Temporal distance gives everyone an opportunity to calm down. The combination of spatial and temporal distance can help Officer Thomas take control of the dispute by giving her a spatial and temporal buffer against physical threats and menacing behavior (Ladd, 2005).

Venting — When people are making physical threats or are practicing menacing behavior, they are capable of saying or doing almost anything. This is especially true within a climate of anger that usually exists when law enforcement officers respond to these types of calls. A law enforcement officer who believes it is important to separate both parties and give them time to calm down may also benefit by allowing the parties to vent their anger directly at the law enforcement officer. There are some distinct advantages in making this decision (Ladd, 2005):

- Whatever physical threats made to the other party becomes more difficult to make directly to a law enforcement officer.

- The law enforcement officer can let them vent their feelings without having the emotional investment in the dispute.

- The law enforcement officer can use their venting as a way of achieving temporal distance.

- The law enforcement officer is viewed as a peacemaker, and not someone only interested in an arrest.

Pacing — Law enforcement officers may assume that controlling the stress of other people in a dispute is one of their first priorities. However, research has demonstrated that by controlling law enforcement officer's personal stress, it is possible to pace others down to the pace of the law enforcement officer, in order to gain control over the dispute (Ladd, 2005). In the case study, if Officer Thomas begins to:

- Lower her tone of voice.

- Breath more slowly encouraging others, to breath more slowly.

- Directly look at those in dispute in order to control the pace of their comments.

- Notice when others have paced themselves down to discuss their dispute and then negotiate terms to end the dispute.

Pacing can be effective because it allows the law enforcement officer an opportunity to gain control over threatening and menacing behavior. It helps an unreasonable dispute achieve more reasonable behavior.

Ground Rules — Law enforcement officers may want to consider setting up ground rules between parties where physical threats and menacing behavior are present (Beers, 1997). Remember, we are assuming in this chapter, that people like George, in the case study, have not yet committed assault (section 120.10 NYS Penal Code) and they still have the opportunity to modify their behavior without having injured someone physically. In fact, it may be important to set up ground rules between parties so that assault is not the final outcome. For example, in the case study, if Officer Thomas has successfully separated George and Martha and has allowed them time to vent their feelings and has successfully paced them down to reasonable thinking and behavior, then her ability to establish ground rules on arguing may save George from being charged with assault and Martha from being a victim of assault. Here are some possible ground rules they can establish when the interactions between them creates a climate of possible physical threats or menacing behavior:

- Have a ground rule that arguing over a problem does not mean they have to attack each other, personally.

- Agree to keep foul language and name-calling out of their discussions. Such language encourages a climate of physical threats and menacing behavior.

- Agree that, if they want to explode with anger against the other person, they will first get physical or temporal distance before sharing their different points of view.

- Agree that they will keep the argument confidential and not look for others to egg them on.

- Agree that if the dispute appears to be headed toward physical threats and menacing behavior that both parties will agree to call some professional person to conciliate the dispute, possibly a law enforcement officer.

Mediation Regarding Orders of Protection — Occasions arise where physical threats and menacing behavior between two parties has resulted in an order of protection where one party has been granted protection from the courts against the other party's behavior (Mosten, 1997). One option that a law enforcement officer has when the threatening party breaks an order of protection, is to charge the party with menacing in the 2nd degree which holds the penalty of a class A misdemeanor. In the case study, Officer Thomas may be informed that Martha has an order of protection against George and that his threatening behavior at her home may warrant an arrest. However experience shows that people who have a history with each other may find it difficult to break old habits. For example, Martha may know the exact "buzz words" that puts George into a rage, causing him to slam the phone and rush to Martha's house with the intent of committing physical injury. On the other hand, George may know exactly when Martha is at her weakest moments and use physical threats or menacing behavior to get his way in an argument. When either of these possibilities happens, arresting someone may satisfy the courts under the law but may not necessarily curtail either party's behavior.

In such cases, Officer Thomas has an alternative option. If George and Martha both agree, Officer Thomas can get the court to temporarily lift the order of protection so that issues surrounding their dispute can be mediated. Issues such as:

- How to talk in front of the children.

- How to vent their feelings without upsetting the other party.

- How to keep the other party informed of each other's behavior.

- How to curtail physical threats and menacing behavior.

- How to work toward lifting the order of protection and both parties being civil with each other.

- How to reconcile secrets, hidden agendas and damaging gossip causing a climate of physical threats and menacing behavior.

The recidivism rates for disputes that end in physical threats or menacing behavior can be as high as 70%. Mediation may be an alternative approach that can resolve many of the common practices that lead to an arrest. Furthermore, both parties agreeing to temporarily lifting of an order of protection to participate in mediation does not mean the order cannot be reinstated. An order of protection and mediation both can be used to protect the rights of citizens who experience physical threats or menacing behavior.

Exercises

Responding to the Case Study (How would Officer Thomas respond to this physical threats and menacing call from a *legal point of view?*)

Responding to the Case Study (How would Officer Thomas respond to this physical threat and menacing call from a *conflict resolution point of view?*)

How many options does Officer Thomas have from a legal point of view?

If selecting a conflict resolution stance to the physical threat and menacing call, Officer Thomas could use what skills?

How can mediation respond to orders of protection?

How could getting distance contribute to resolving physical threats and menacing cases?

How could the ground rules help resolving physical threats and menacing behavior cases?

When is an appropriate time to use pacing as a conflict resolution skill in cases of physical threats and menacing behavior?

Chapter 3

PETIT LARCENY: SHOPLIFTING

Introduction

P etit larceny can be defined as intentionally stealing, taking or carrying away personal goods or property, with a value of less than $250, owned by another person (Rosen, 2004). However, the $250 is an average and can vary from State to State. The threshold for what is classified as petit larceny v grand larceny, depending on the state statutes, could be $250.00 for petit larceny or as inflation occurs as high as $500.00. Regardless of the financial limit, petit larceny is a major problem in the United States, especially with youthful offenders.

Petit larceny represents a major portion of the juvenile crime problems facing our country. Youths charged with property offenses represent more than 40% of all juvenile arrests and approximately 50% of all delinquency cases referred to U.S. juvenile courts (Snyder, 2000). A recent analysis of approximately one million juvenile court records across nearly 2,000 jurisdictions (serving over 76% of the U.S. juvenile population) revealed that shoplifting was the most common juvenile court referral for youths under age 15, accounting for almost 25% of all property offense petitions (Sickmund, 2000).

However, youthful offenders are not the only group that is guilty of shoplifting. Petit larceny is not restricted to youths as there is a proportionate share of elderly people that steal and statistics are rampant with the notion that employee theft may exceed customer theft, yet there is little publicity for employee thefts, since they try to protect their name and thus avoid reporting and merely fire the employee.

Beyond the actual act of stealing, frustration may occur for police officers when some retailers have a policy not to prosecute. When the merchandiser detects or has suspicion that someone is stealing a product, their reaction is to confront the thief and ask them to return the item before they leave the store. Some invoke a ban and tell the thief not to return. The down side of this reaction is that the word gets out that certain retailers have a "non-prosecutorial" stance and they become "fair game," for the shoplifters. This can result in a "non-response" when and if they receive a call from Mall Security that a person is apprehended and they discover items stolen, without a receipt, from a non-prosecutorial store. Keeping this in mind, the following is an overview of laws on petit larceny and specifically shoplifting that should be considered when responding to a call where stealing of property is involved:

Legal Criteria and Shoplifting

Shoplifting complaints combine different sections of many State Penal Codes when considering a response by law enforcement officers. In this section, we will consider some of those variables and look at numerous criteria that may or may not change an officer's thinking when responding to a shoplifting complaint. The following represents basic criteria to consider when responding to these complaints:

Grand Larceny vs. Petit Larceny

The term larceny is synonymous with the term theft and is defined as a taking with the intent to permanently deprive the owner of the item stolen (Virginia Code §§ 18.2-95 to 18.2-96). Another definition of larceny is wrongfully taking, obtaining or withholding of another's property (Section 155.05 of the New York State Penal Law). Regardless of how each particular State defines larceny, the basic criteria for larceny is understood as the act of someone stealing from another.

Petit larceny generally follows the same criteria found under these definitions of larceny, but the dollar amount is one of the criteria that will identify a theft as petit larceny rather than larceny. In New York State, the main distinction between the two is the value of the item taken. In New York State the value is $250 between petit larceny and grand larceny. While in Virginia, larceny of an item with a value of $200 or more is considered grand larceny while a value of less than $200 is considered petit larceny.

Petit Larceny as a Misdemeanor

A person who commits petit larceny is guilty of a misdemeanor in most States. In addition to any other penalty, the court shall order the person to pay restitution. If you are arrested for shoplifting, it can be a serious crime which can be a misdemeanor or a felony, depending on the item taken. For example, petit larceny, which is stealing an item worth less than a certain dollar amount, is a misdemeanor. Over that amount, the offense is grand theft, which is a felony. The dollar amounts that determine petit larceny or grand theft vary from state to state.

Both misdemeanors and felonies may be punishable by confinement in jail or a fine. While a judge may order probation or another sentence not involving confinement, a person accused of shoplifting should not necessarily expect to avoid criminal prosecution by payment of restitution to the merchant (Homant, Kelly & Kennedy, 2003).

Shoplifting: Probable Cause

Here are six important questions to ask the owner of a store where shoplifting may have taken place (McGoey, 1990):

- Did you see the shoplifter approach your merchandise?

- Did you see the shoplifter select your merchandise?

- Did you see the shoplifter conceal, carry away or convert your merchandise?

- Did you maintain continuous observation of the shoplifter?

- Did you see the shoplifter fail to pay for the merchandise?

- Did you approach the shoplifter outside of the store?

It is important that store employees actually see shoplifters approach their merchandise and select it. Sometimes, customers may have brought merchandise back into a store for exchange and can be wrongfully accused of shoplifting. It is important for law enforcement officers to establish that the shoplifter openly concealed the merchandise, did not pay for it and left the store with it in his or her possession.

Shoplifting: Detention

Some states have "Merchant Statutes" that give the store operator some limited liability protection if they approach a suspected shoplifter in good faith and the stop is based on a reasonable belief that shoplifting had occurred. In these states, a statute has been written that allows merchants to hold a potential shoplifter for a temporary period of time. This can be for recovering the merchandise or summoning the police (McGoey, 1990). To detain someone, under the statute, means that they are not technically under arrest, but merely being temporarily investigated.

In jurisdictions that do not have the protection of a merchant's statute, a store operator must make a citizen's arrest without any liability protection. In most states, to make a citizen's arrest, you must see the crime (misdemeanor) committed in your presence, or in the case of a felony, committed outside of your presence, you must be certain that the crime actually occurred (Ohlin & Stauber, 200).

Case Study

The store manager met Officer Shaw at the front door of the department store and asked if they could talk first before meeting Janice, who was caught stealing beauty supplies from the cosmetic counter. It seemed that Bill, the store manager, wanted to discuss Janice's future; along with, what were the legal ramifications for the department store. Bill directed Officer Shaw to a private room where he could discuss the complaint before the Officer talked to Janice.

Officer Shaw agreed to his request. He knew that Bill needed to give him more information before approaching Janice and he, also, wanted to ask Bill specific questions to determine the severity of the crime. First, Officer Shaw knew that he had a case of larceny or petit larceny. However, Officer Shaw wanted to know specific information that would influence his conversation with Janice. Here are examples of the questions asked by Officer Shaw to Bill, the store manager.

- How much was the property worth?

- Has she damaged the property?

- Were others involved that would indicate a pattern of stealing?

- How did the larceny complaint harm the store in general?

Officer Shaw wanted Bill to know that there were two realities to consider when weighing prosecution of this case. First of all, he informed Bill that his store did not want to get a reputation for a lack of prosecution that would encourage other shoplifters to mark his store for theft. However, Bill indicated that he wanted to consider the store's reputation and did not want the petit larceny complaint to harm his store financially. Keeping these two thoughts in mind, Officer Shaw went into the adjacent office to confront Janice.

When Officer Shaw entered the room where Janice was being detained, he went through the checklist in his mind:

☐ "How much was this property worth?"
☐ "Has she damaged the property?"
☐ "Were there others involved that would indicate a pattern of stealing?"
☐ "How did the petit larceny complaint harm the store in general?"

As it turned out, Janice was a sixteen-year-old who had never been in trouble before. Officer Shaw found her anxious and afraid of what was going to happen next. After interviewing Janice, he would return to Bill and ask him whether he wanted to prosecute or not. He would share with Bill that Janice was very cooperative and answered his questions directly and honestly as much as he could tell. After hearing Officer Shaw's statement, Bill, asked if there was anything that could be done beyond returning the merchandise. Officer Shaw said that he might want to consider other methods for dealing with Janice's offense other than charging her with a misdemeanor.

In some of these cases conflict resolution skills may be a viable alternative to court action that may deter Janice from future shoplifting behavior. The following criteria may be important to consider when responding to this and other shoplifting cases where petit larceny needs the expertise of a law enforcement officer who understands the law regarding shoplifting and has conflict resolution skills that may prevent such thefts from happening in the first place:

Conflict Resolution and Shoplifting

In reviewing the legal criteria to consider when responding to shoplifting, it may be important that the officer understand he or she is not responding to a complaint where grand larceny has been committed and is not responding to employee theft. The officer is responding to a petit larceny complaint dealing with shoplifting and may have certain latitude in helping the store owner discover alternative conflict resolution methods for processing these com-plaints. Also, conflict resolution skills probably should not be con-sidered with an organized group of shoplifters who make stealing a business. The following skills address those individuals who fall into the category of people who commit petit larceny crimes such as, misguided youth, adults with no criminal records or individuals suffering from anxiety, depression or any other counseling problem that causes impulsive behavior. In these cases being charged with a misdemeanor may cause more serious crimes at a future date (Lane, 2003) and increase the rate of recidivism for the officer and the store. Keeping this in mind, conflict resolution skills may be a viable alternative to court action that may deter individuals from future shoplifting or other petit larceny crimes.

The Importance of an Apology

Here is a conflict resolution skill that, at first, may appear to a law enforcement officer as overly naïve for a shoplifter to believe, giving an apology to a store owner will change his or her behavior. For example, in the case study, for Officer Shaw to ask Janice to simply go into Bill, the store owner, and apologize may appear to have little benefit for all three of them. However, if Officer Shaw helps Janice form her apology, then such an act could have beneficial consequences for the store owner, Janice and the community in which Officer Shaw patrols. Here are criteria to consider in helping shoplifters committing petit larceny in apologizing for stealing another's property:

Making Amends – Somewhere in the apology the shoplifter should offer some form of reparation and amends. Actual behavior can make the apology more valuable to both the shoplifter and the store owner. Within this offer, the shoplifter should specifically agree to do something for the store owner. By making a positive request, the shoplifter can help balance out the negative impact of the act of petit larceny. When you consider that only 10% of shoplifters are professional thieves and most shoplifting is performed by people suffering from emotional or psychological disturbances in their lives, then making amends takes on a higher priority for concerned law enforcement (Weinberg, 1995). Reparations have a tendency to help balance out what is "fair" when property owners and shoplifters meet after a crime is committed. A law enforcement officer can help shoplifters formulate exactly what they want to say when confronting the property owner. Face to face confrontation puts the onus of responsibility on the offender while giving the victim an opportunity to address the shoplifter directly.

Being Specific – If the law enforcement officer takes this approach of helping the offender to make an apology, then being specific about the apology may give it more value. For example, in mediation sessions, agreements that are stated in general or vague terms have less of a chance for success than those that are made more specific (Mayer, 2003). The same rules apply when making an apology. The more specific the apology the higher chance for it being effective. Here are guidelines to consider when helping a shoplifter make an apology to a property owner.

- Make the shoplifter state what has been stolen and how much the item or items are worth.

- Have the shoplifter give a reason for their shoplifting, no matter how difficult it may be to state a reason.

- Have the shoplifter ask what they can do to make amends for their behavior.

- Have the shoplifter state to the property owner what they may be willing to do to make amends.

- Have the shoplifter form an apology; not based on avoiding arrest but based on remorse for what has been stolen.

Community Service

Sometimes law enforcement officers can influence the district attorney or the judge when shoplifters are arrested for petit larceny if the law enforcement officer believes some form of community service would better serve the shoplifter, the property owner and the community. The following are issues to consider when recommending community service as a remedy for the crime of shoplifting:

- **Worthwhile Work** – Someone given community service should be given an explanation of why this work is worthwhile to the community. Even if law enforcement officers arrest shoplifters for petit larceny. It does not have to mean they have finished their relationship with these offenders. They may be in a position to act as mentors for some of the youthful offenders who commit shoplifting or they may show adults how community service can be beneficial for everyone. However, in order to be successful with community service, the work should have some value to the community such as, helping with improvements to a playground for youth or helping to disseminate literature on AIDS prevention.

- **The Importance of Closure** – Whenever possible, projects should be designed to have a clear beginning and end. In this way offenders can see firsthand the impact of their efforts. Seeing a project through completion boosts personal satisfaction and can provide a complete learning experience about the benefits of community service. In the case study, Janice would probably benefit more from a worthwhile project that helps her community where she sees the project through to the end, than for Officer Shaw to charge her with a misdemeanor. If Janice can find closure to a meaningful project, then she has a higher probability in finding closure to her shoplifting.

- **Focus on Helping the Disadvantaged** – There is a special atmosphere surrounding community service projects that benefit the disadvantaged. Something seems to click with offenders when they help at Special Olympics events, work in community kitchens or build homeless shelters. Perhaps it has something to do with the role reversal – they are doing something for someone less fortunate. In the case study, Officer Shaw may have an opportunity to help Janice understand what it means to be less fortunate and discover that her shoplifting adds to the conflicts in her community. Helping those less fortunate may be her opportunity to add to the growth of her community rather than its demise.

Counseling Issues and Shoplifting

It may be important to reiterate that only about 10% of shoplifters are professional thieves. Most people who shoplift are usually suffering from some emotional difficulty. Sometimes people steal as a way to gain social acceptance (Rourke, 1995). Others are experiencing tension or depression, usually in relationships with significant others (Applebaum & Klemmer, 1988). Professionals state that some shoplifters have poor impulse control (Damon, 1988), while some believe that there is a phenomenon known as being a "shopaholic." (Damon, 1988). The following are some counseling issues that a law enforcement officer should consider when deciding on using some form of conflict resolution in petit larceny cases regarding shoplifting:

- **Social Acceptance** – Peer pressure can be at the root of many shoplifting experiences whether you are a teenager or an adult. The envy of seeing friends or others in society with objects that signify success can influence some individuals to steal from establishments that sell these items. This is especially prominent with teenage shoplifters who are looking for social acceptance among their peers. Law enforcement officers do not have to be counselors or therapists to point out other ways of achieving social acceptance without practicing shoplifting. In the case study, Officer Shaw may want to ask Janice the question, "How has shoplifting helped you gain social acceptance with your friends?"

- **Stress and Shoplifting** – Shoplifting can be an impulsive act for those who are under too much stress. It can be a way to relieve one's psychological tensions. Some may describe shoplifters as addicted to shopping where they have poor impulse control and find they cannot stop shopping and steal, in order to fulfill their addictive impulses. In the case study, Officer Shaw may ask Janice what kind of stress she is under in her life and what she can do to relieve her stress. He may recommend she go to counseling to find out how to relieve her specific stress or he may point out the added stress that may accompany being arrested for petit larceny and a possible misdemeanor. Though it is not Officer Shaw's responsibility to treat Janice's stress, an understanding of her emotional state may help him in making the most effective decision regarding her future. Here are other stress related issues that a law enforcement officer should consider when interviewing someone who has committed the crime of shoplifting – Depression, Unfulfilled Sexual Gratification, Revenge against Others and Envy against Others (Gottfredson & Hirschi, 1990).

- **Excitement and Shoplifting** – Some shoplifters commit crimes because of the excitement they experience when stealing property from another. Some have stated that they experience a certain "rush" when entering a store and secretly stealing while in the presence of store personnel (Hiew, 1981). This often can be seen with teenage shoplifting. Developmentally, adolescence is a period of rebellion and ex-perimentation and shoplifting can be one method for rebelling and experimenting that can be connected to other forms of rebellion and experimentation. For example, experimenting with drugs and shoplifting can be associated with the same form of excitement that comes with such experimentation. For example, in the case study, it may be important to find out whether Janice finds her shoplifting exciting and is she using drugs concurrently with stealing to experience excitement. If this turns out to be the case, counseling may not be the most advantageous approach to her problem. In this case it may be important to arrest Janice and charge her with a misdemeanor in order to make petit larceny less exciting.

Communities and Shoplifting

There is a growing trend in some communities that one way to stop shoplifting is to offer awareness programs about the effects of shoplifting on the community, the family and the individual (Blakely & Gibbs, 2000). Law enforcement can play a major role in such prevention techniques by offering presentations to schools and community agencies that show the vital statistics on the consequences of shoplifting to the entire community. Such programs have grown in popularity and work from the beliefs that to stop shoplifting may require a complete community effort. Here is a chance for business, law enforcement and families to work closely with each other with a crime that is not necessarily acted out by hardened criminals. Most shoplifters are everyday citizens who have social acceptance issues or are under some form of emotional and psychological stress. Community programs can change the way law enforcement approaches shoplifting by empowering others to understand the warning signals for shoplifting behavior and intervene before a pattern of theft takes hold in a community. Here are some warning signs for communities to consider when making the public aware of shoplifting in their neighborhoods (Homant, Kelly & Kennedy, 2003):

- **Get to know the people who operate the neighboring businesses.** They are your neighbors for eight or more hours a day. Making personal contact is the best way to get acquainted. Make an effort to introduce yourself to others – nearby residents, schools, civic groups, libraries, clubs – in the neighborhood.

- **Watch and report.** Report suspicious behavior to law enforcement immediately, even if it means taking a chance on being wrong. A telephone tree is an effective means of sharing information with other merchants. Should a problem develop, each merchant is responsible for calling one or two others on the tree.

- **Secure your property.** Contact your local police or sheriff's department to conduct a security survey of your business.

Ask for their advice on lights, alarms, locks, and other security measures.

- **Engrave all valuable office equipment and tools.** Use an identification number – a tax identification number, license, or other unique number. Check with law enforcement for their recommendation.

- **Aggressively advertise your Business Watch group.** Post signs and stickers saying that your block of businesses is organized to prevent crime by watching out for and reporting suspicious activities to law enforcement.

Exercises

Responding to the Case Study (How would Officer Shaw respond to this shoplifting call from a *legal point of view?*)

Responding to the Case Study (How would Officer Shaw respond to this shoplifting call from a *conflict resolution point of view?*)

How many options does Officer Shaw have from a legal point of view?

If selecting a conflict resolution stance to the shoplifting call, Officer Shaw could use what skills?

How can apologizing help the shoplifter stop his or her behavior?

How can a shoplifter be specific when making amends?

What would you consider worthwhile community service for shoplifting?

When would you suggest a shoplifter seek counseling?

Chapter 4

CUSTODY & VISITATION

Introduction

U ntil about twenty-five years ago, custody of a divorcing couple's children was, by statute, presumptively awarded to the children's mother. The "tender years doctrine," a tenet of family law for more than 100 years, required that young children be kept with their mothers after divorce. The basis for this mandate was the widely held belief that women were more "naturally suited" to parenthood than men (Bloomer, Ruedt & Sipe, 2002). It was not until the early 1970s that a political commitment to racial and gender equality forced the repeal of the tender years doctrine. New custody laws enacted across the United States declared that "the best interests of the children" must be the primary consideration in custody decisions (Dachman & Leving, 1997).

This has had dramatic implications for custody and visitation entering into the 21st Century. For example, in the early 1960's the most frequently cited factor to be considered in custody decisions was "motherhood." In today's society, the factor of "motherhood" is hardly mentioned. This has given mothers and fathers equal footing when considering custody and visitation issues and it complicates the role of law enforcement in determining what factors to consider when going on a call regarding a custody and visitation dispute. Unlike divorce, child custody is not a legal event that can be negotiated or fought over and ultimately settled within a year or two. Legal custody lasts until the child reaches adulthood (Mason, 2000) and within this period of time conflict between the divorced couples can find an officer on call for some form of custody or visitation dispute.

This has many states advocating for "joint custody" where responsibility for children is shared and with the hope of reducing any prejudice between men and women. However, in reality, joint custody has not lessened the burden for law enforcement—which may be the first line of intervention when these custody and visitation issues break down (Mills, 1999).

Legal Criteria and Custody and Visitation

When looking at the legal aspects of custody and visitation across the United States, it is safe to say that most States base their decisions in custody issues on what is in the "best interest of the children." However, there is no actual definition of this phrase found in the legal criteria of different States regarding custody and visitation. In most States, there is no automatic or prima facie right of either parent to custody, yet for the most part, the custodial parent in many States is most often the mother and, also, many States grant reasonable visitation to grandparents (Slade, 2000).

Best Interest of the Child

Different States define the best interest of the child in many different ways but the following list captures some of the criteria needed to identify custody and visitation rights for couples (Oberlander, 1995):

- The parenting skills of each parent.

- Who has been the primary caregiver?

- The mental and physical health of family members.

- Parental history and the need of the child to live in an environment that is stable.

- The ability of each parent to cooperate with each other.

- Child care and work schedules.

- The interactions with siblings and other extended family members.

Types of Custody

There are three major types of custody that law enforcement officers should be aware of when meeting a call in a custody and visitation complaint, namely (Friedman, 1995):

- **Sole Custody** – This is where the children have a primary residence with one parent along with this parent having major decision-making power regarding: education, health, religion, and other activities. The non-custodial parent may have the right to consult with the custodial parent but does not have responsibility for their care. Also, the non-custodial parent may have input on visitation, yet must confer with the custodial parent.

- **Joint Custody** – In these cases, children reside with one parent or with both parents and share joint decision-making on major issues such as education, health, religion and activities. Child support would be equalized between both parents with the lower income parent in accordance with guidelines on child support.

- **Split Custody** – Some States warrant split custody arrangements in rare cases with extenuating circumstances. Split custody is the term used to describe circumstances where one or more children will live primarily with each parent. However, such cases are usually put to strict assessment as to what is in the best interests of the child.

Uniform Child Custody Jurisdiction Act

With the increase in mobility, separating couples do not necessarily stay in one place. This forced the federal government to create the Uniform Child Custody Jurisdiction Act (Federal Government, 1968). This act states that, "courts of the various States involved should cooperate to figure out what court is the most appropriate to hear a custody case." Under the Uniform Custody Jurisdiction Act, a State's court will hear the case if any of the following are true:

- The state is the child's home state.

- The state had been the child's home state within six months before the case started, and the child was moved out of state, and a parent or someone acting as a parent lives in the state.

- It is in the best interest of the child for the court to take the case because the child and at least one parent have a significant connection to the state.

- The child is present in the state and there is some kind of emergency, such as an abusive parent or neglect.

- It appears that no other state will take the case and it is in the best interest of the child that the court do so.

Note: The Uniform Child Custody Jurisdiction Act was created to unify states on custody and visitation issues. However, most states have found ways to repeal or change portions of this Act in accordance with their state held legislation and beliefs. It may be important for law enforcement officers to understand their state's interpretation of child custody jurisdiction when responding to a custody and visitation call.

Case Study

Thelma and Bob had a custody and visitation agreement where the two children lived with Thelma, and Bob would pick them up every other weekend after school and they would go over to Bob's house every Wednesday night. This agreement had been in place for over a year and it seemed to be working until the incident that happened at 5 pm, on the night of October 11th.

Officer Blake was asked to respond to a call at Thelma's residence where a dispute was taking place between Bob and Thelma over Bob's right to visitation this particular weekend. Upon Officer Blake's arrival, Bob rushed to him with his custody and visitation agreement in hand, demanding that Thelma turn over the two children for the weekend. In a calm and collected manner, Officer Blake asked if Bob would refrain from any more outbursts until he had an opportunity to understand the situation.

First of all, Officer Blake checked to see if any signs of child abuse, neglect or domestic violence was evident. He asked if he could see the children and, after a brief discussion, it was determined that the children were healthy and well cared for, thus eliminating any domestic violence evidence directed at either of the children's parents.

Next, Officer Blake questioned Thelma's refusal to give over the children when it was clear that a specific custody and visitation agreement had been signed by the judge giving Bob his visitation rights every other weekend. Thelma's response to him convinced Officer Blake that he had a conflict resolution problem rather than a legal problem to contend with regarding Bob and Thelma's dispute.

As it turned out, one of Bob and Thelma's children was sick with the flu and she believed that it was mandatory that he stay in his bed at her house. Beyond this, the other younger boy felt uncomfortable going to Bob's house without his older brother – a pattern they had been practicing for the last year.

It was obvious to Officer Blake that something should be done to resolve this dispute. It was now past 5pm and he knew that lawyers and other court personnel at the courthouse had left for the day and that it would be up to him to help this couple maintain a sense of civility for themselves and their children.

After some reflection, Officer Blake decided to mediate the dispute between Bob and Thelma. He already had a reasonable understanding of their initial issues and decided that some form of reconciliation was better than making a judgment on how the visitation schedule should be fulfilled this particular Friday evening. He knew that Bob wanted to uphold the signed custody and visitation agreement and Thelma, on the other hand, wanted Bob to agree to common sense when one of the children was sick and in her opinion, could not be moved.

The following criteria may be important to consider when responding to this and other custody and visitation cases where dispute resolution needs the expertise of a law enforcement officer who understands the nuances of custody and visitation and has conflict resolution skills that may prevent such events turning into more serious problems such as abuse or domestic violence.

Conflict Resolution and Custody and Visitation

In responding to a complaint where custody and visitation issues are present, it is first important to the responding officer to rule out child abuse and domestic violence issues that may change the officer's resolution of the complaint. The following questions may be of value before attempting conflict resolution with both partners (Fagan, 1996):

- Do you have any concerns about resolving this problem in the same room together with your spouse?

- Are you fearful of your spouse for any reason?

- Has your spouse threatened to hurt you in any way?

- Have you ever called the police, requested protection from abuse or sought help for yourself as a result of abuse by your spouse?

- Are you currently afraid that your spouse will physically harm you?

- Do you believe that you will be able to communicate with your spouse on an equal basis?

- Has your partner ever threatened to deny you access to your children?

- Has the Department of Children and Family Services ever been involved with your family?

In all of these questions, the officer has the opportunity to rule out more serious crimes before attempting some form of conflict resolution. Without such guidelines, it may be difficult for the officer to determine if both partners are of good will when attempting to resolve a dispute. On the other hand, if domestic violence and child abuse issues are ruled out and the officer believes conflict resolution is possible, then it may be in the best interest of the couple, the officer, and the community if the dispute is resolved before it turns into more serious matters (Garrity & Baris, 1994).

The Importance of Neutrality — It is important for the law enforcement officer to maintain a sense of neutrality when trying to resolve conflict between fighting spouses. For example, in the case study, Officer Blake must assure Thelma that the fact that he is also a male does not mean that he will be favoring Bob in discussions to resolve the visitation dispute. If Officer Blake has previously talked to one of the disputants then he must make sure the other can continue to see him as neutral and finally, it may be important for both Thelma and Bob to openly declare that they both believe that Officer Blake can remain neutral during their discussion over the visitation incident. In order to create neutrality, Officer Blake may need to establish the following criteria (Ladd, 2005):

- **Spatial Balance** – It may be important that officers who attempt conflict resolution with disputing spouses realize that spatially favoring one spouse over another can cause a loss of neutrality where one spouse feels you are favoring the other based solely on where you stand. For example, if Officer Blake stands next to Bob during discussions regarding Thelma and Bob's dispute over visitation, then Thelma may believe that Officer Blake favors Bob based solely on where he stands. Even if it means that Officer Blake has to move back and forth between the two, the loss of neutrality by spatially favoring one person over the other may end the chances for reconciliation before dispute resolution begins.

- **Temporal Balance** – Even though it may seem awkward, making sure that both spouses have equal time to speak may be as important as what they are saying. One of the dangers in letting both sides describe the dispute is when one of the spouses wants to go into a long history of:

The relationship and not deal with the immediate problem at hand. For example, in the case study, it is important that both Thelma and Bob have equal time to say what is on their minds. However, if one of them gets into a long story about their problems, then Officer Blake may be seen by the other as favoring the story teller, for the mere fact that he or she is monopolizing the conversation. It is important to stay neutral by giving both parties equal time to speak, but not to let one party do all of the speaking.

Changing Accusations into Requests — A useful technique to use when one spouse begins to make accusations about the behavior of the other is to turn the accusations into requests for the future (Sapsonek, 1983). For example, in the case study, instead of Bob showing his custody and visitation agreement and demanding he have the children for the weekend, Officer Blake could help him make a request in the future that: when Thelma wants to alter the agreement, that she give Bob ample notice to consider his position regarding her request. Also, instead of Thelma chastising Bob for not having any common sense when it came to the physical condition of their children, she could make a future request that they develop plans for visitation if or when the children become ill. If Officer Blake can change both Bob and Thelma's accusations to requests, then he has directed them to a workable agreement that helps: the police department to lessen similar chronic calls, the community by using the police for more serious offenses and Thelma and Bob for finding creative ways to love their children.

Refocusing the Problem — A series of negative comments by both sides can turn a custody and visitation call into an out of control shouting match where neither side wins and the children may become the ultimate losers. A law enforcement officer responding to a call where there is an escalating pattern of emotional conflict can refocus the problem by talking about some of the more positive aspects of their relationship even during a visitation visit. For example, if Bob and Thelma begin to yell at each other, Officer Blake can refocus their attention to talking about how they both love their children or how for the last year the visitation schedule has worked. In either of these examples, the spouses need to de-escalate their emotions in order to agree that visitation has for the most part worked and can be accomplished by refocusing the problem onto something else. If child abuse and domestic violence are not the issue, most conflicts between spouses concerning custody and visitation are usually over some misunderstanding or some form of confusion.

Altering the Visitation Schedule

For those law enforcement officers who help spouses with altering their visitation agreements, the following items must be given consideration (Bush and Folger, 1994): (Note: Agreements made are temporary and eventually need approval by the Courts.)

- **Clarity** – Any changes in visitation must be clear and make sense to the spouses and there probably should be no confusing legal terms used. As long as the law enforcement officer does not change the agreed upon days for visitation, then changing times and circumstances that both parties agree on can only benefit the visitation schedule. For example, if Bob and Thelma agree that Bob will pick the children up after 5 pm on Fridays every other week instead of after school at 3 pm, then they may agree that between five and three both sides can determine any extenuating circumstances that may arise unexpectedly. Law enforcement officers can be the front line in making these minor changes that make a visitation agreement work. The key word is "clarity." When agreements are clear, there is a higher probability that people will follow these agreements.

- **Specificity** – If changes are made in a visitation schedule by a law enforcement officer, the more specific the changes to more lasting the agreement. Numerous calls based on custody and visitation may develop because the original visitation schedule was not specific enough. Here are some guidelines for helping spouses specifically refine their visitation schedules:

    1. Who has greater access to being with the children?
    2. What residence is most desirable for housing the children?
    3. What specifically has been decided on holidays and vacations?
    4. Who may be moving in the near future?
    5. How are we going to specifically communicate changes in the visitation schedule?
    6. What conflicts may specifically cause problems in the future regarding the visitation schedules?

Power Imbalances

Any law enforcement officer that answers a call regarding custody or visitation should consider the power imbalances that take place between spouses who are in dispute. These power imbalances can take on different behaviors and law enforcement should be aware of these imbalances. Here are some of the power imbalances that law enforcement officers may encounter when answering a call (Blau, 1994):

- **Physical Power Imbalances** – One of the problems that face law enforcement when responding to a custody and visitation call is that one has to keep in the back of his or her mind that one of the parties may be stronger or bigger than the other and that one means that spouses solve problems is to use force. In the case study, Bob decided to call the police to resolve his dispute with Thelma. However, others may take power into their own hands and escalate the dispute. At this point, domestic violence is always a possibility and when you enter this domain conflict resolution usually does not become an alternative. It is not advocated that conflict resolution be used in most domestic violence cases.

- **Communication Power Imbalances** – Sometimes power imbalances are found in the act of communication taking place between two disputing spouses. For whatever reasons, one spouse may be more articulate than the other. In these cases, a law enforcement officer may have to help the less articulate party express his or her point of view in order to negotiate a new visitations schedule. Sometimes this help will come in the form of re-framing what the person is trying to say. For example, in the case study, Thelma may be less articulate than Bob in making the point that one of the children should not be moved while ill. Officer Blake may take what Thelma is trying to say and re-frame it in such a way that Bob understands her statement. Here is an example from the case study:

  Thelma talking to Bob: Don't you have any common sense? You must be stupid to think that your oldest son must go with you this weekend.

  Officer Blake re-framing for Thelma: What Thelma is trying to say is that it may not be in your son's best interest to stay with the visitation schedule this weekend.

By Officer Blake re-framing the statements of Thelma, Bob is more amenable to listening to her. The communication power imbalance can be overcome by the law enforcement officer understanding the basic communication skill of re-framing. Here are other conflict resolution skills to consider when facing power imbalances in custody and visitation disputes (Klienman & Mandell, 1996):

- *Identify power plays as counterproductive.* Many power plays are a form of posturing – i.e., getting the upper hand. They are not very productive ways of behaving when trying to resolve a dispute.

- *Compensate for either party's low level of negotiating skills by slowing down the process, clarifying issues and options.* If this is not sufficient, suggest outside support, for example, counselors, neighborhood advocates or social workers.

- *Interrupt any intimidating patterns*; identify intimidating statements as inappropriate, restate the goals of both spouses.

- *Remember that resolving disputes based on fear are not disputes that may stay resolved for a long period of time.* Power imbalances sometimes have one weaker party agree based on fear of the other party. Law enforcement officers that help in resolving custody and visitation disputes should watch for agreements being made out of one spouse's fear of the other.

Exercises

Responding to the Case Study (How would Officer Blake respond to the case study custody and visitation call from a *legal point of view?*)

Responding to the Case Study (How would Officer Blake respond to the case study custody and visitation call from a *conflict resolution point of view?*)

How many options does Officer Blake have from a legal point of view?

If selecting a conflict resolution stance to the custody and visitation call, Officer Blake could use what skills?

How can Officer Blake rule out domestic violence issues in responding to Bob and Thelma's dispute?

What is the importance of neutrality in resolving the dispute between Bob and Thelma?

What could be the importance of changing accusations into requests?

What should Officer Blake do if he discovers a communication power imbalance between Bob and Thelma?

Chapter 5

DISTURBING THE PEACE (NOISE)

Introduction

An issue that law enforcement is facing in the 21st Century is the increasing level of noise that has permeated our communities. Ordinances have been established in all of our major cities and smaller communities have raised the issue of whether noise is a law enforcement issue that leads to more serious crime, such as physical assault and harassment (Brinkman & Kirtchner, 1994). The world is becoming a more crowded place and along with it the potential for disturbing the peace becomes an ongoing problem.

Beyond disturbing the peace of others is the personal liability put on our citizens when the decibel levels of noise reach a certain level. In an article entitled, "Clamoring for Quiet: New Ways to Mitigate Noise," John Manuel gives an environmental health perspective on the effects of noise on the general population.

From a law enforcement perspective, disturbing the peace and the noise associated with it, has been an ongoing problem. The closer people live and work together, the more potential for one's peace to be disturbed. Keeping this in mind, it may require a discussion of noise and disturbing the peace in order to render a reasonable response when an officer is required to respond to a call where noise is concerned.

To some, the occasional barking dog complaint my not seem like much of a problem, yet it stands for something far more dangerous. In an age of tension and stress; barking dogs, loud music and constant shouting may be the breaking points for those who have spent a full day of other accumulated tension and these stressors may add to a more serious conflict between neighbors and friends (Gaylin, 2003).

The following will give us an overview of some of the ordinances that currently exist that address disturbing the peace and especially noise. Beyond the overview, we will look at conflict resolution strategies for resolving noise and disturbing the peace.

As we will discover, disturbing the peace is a crime generally defined as the unsettling of proper order in a public space through

59

one's actions. This can include creating loud noise by fighting or challenging to fight, disturbing others by loud and unreasonable noise, or using offensive words likely to incite violence. Disturbing the peace is typically considered a misdemeanor and is often punishable by either a fine or brief term in jail (Looseleaf Law, 2006).

Legal Criteria for Disturbing the Peace

Some of the tenets for defining disturbing the peace can easily fall beyond only loud and unreasonable noise or challenging someone to a fight. Beyond the requirements of disorderly conduct, are those moments when noise and challenges become more serious crimes. The following gives a perspective on how disturbing the peace can escalate into more serious problems for law enforcement:

Disturbing the Peace vs. Disorderly Conduct

In the criminal law of the United States, disorderly conduct is a name given to an offense that usually covers acts that generally disturb the public peace, yet go beyond just noise and undertake some form of physical action against another person. Here is a typical example of how disorderly conduct may be defined according to a typical statutory definition, in this case the statutes pertaining to the State of New York (Looseleaf Law, 2006):

A person who recklessly, knowingly or intentionally:

- Engages in fighting or in tumultuous conduct.

- Makes unreasonable noise and continues to do so after being asked to stop.

- Disrupts a lawful assembly of persons.

- Commits disorderly conduct.

Fighting is perhaps the clearest act within the scope of disorderly conduct. What is tumultuous conduct, or what constitutes unreasonable noise is far harder to decide. So, within the comparison between disturbing the peace and disorderly conduct, many statutes across the United States give police officers and other authorities fairly broad discretion to arrest people whose activities they find undesirable for a wide variety of reasons.

First Amendment and Fourteenth Amendment Rights

The broad interpretation of disturbing the peace and making noise and the act of disorderly conduct has made the court systems across the country, on occasions restrict the broad and vague definitions of these statutes to make certain that freedom of speech and assembly and other forms of protected expression under the First Amendment are not affected.

Also, important in considering disturbing the peace and disorderly conduct, is the consideration under the Fourteenth Amendment that allows for due process rights to be upheld. However, no court has struck down a disorderly conduct statute as being unconstitutionally vague.(Looseleaf Law, 2006)

Under these guidelines, the use of some form of conflict resolution seems a viable alternative with laws that are not necessarily made for an arrest all of the time and must adhere to fairly strict guidelines upheld by the First and the Fourteenth Amendments.

Case Study

The small college town in northern New York is home to two universities. The universities have a small but vocal international student group. The housing for the majority of these students is located off of the campus in the small rural village that is home to the universities. The universities have been in existence for over one hundred years, so their presence is well ingrained into the fabric of the community. It is only recently that the significant international student body has been present in the community.

It has come to the attention of the Dean of Students that there has been conflict brewing over a period of time that has involved the local police force as well as the university police departments. The issue has surrounded the housing in a local apartment complex that includes the majority of the international student population. The languages spoken by the students include: Spanish, Chinese, Arabic and French. The issue specifically is noise as it relates to the customs observed by the students surrounding holidays and other days of celebration for the international students. There have been numerous occasions when the police have been called to ask various groups in the complex to keep the noise level down at certain times when sleeping or studying is going on in the apartment complex.

The Dean of Students of one of the universities has called for a meeting between the local police, campus security, the Housing staff and counseling services (which includes trained mediators). The intent of the meeting is to gather information to go forward in an effort to end the conflicts over noise at the local apartment complex before they escalate into a more serious situation. The meeting was held and brought out the following issues; the local police forces have responded to complaints of noise at the complex on twenty different occasions during the current semester. They reported that they have referred the matters on nearly half of the calls to the campus security forces to follow up on the complaints. Campus security reported that they have assisted local police in responding to the calls when they have involved students enrolled at their university. It seems that the complaints are primarily coming from the French-speaking group and are usually directed at the Chinese students. The main issues of noise involve the Chinese students and their karaoke machine that they play well into the night. The students complain that they are unable to study in the evenings because the sounds of karaoke fill the building into the wee hours of the morning nearly every week night for the past few weeks. They claim that they have attempted to bang on the ceiling, call the noise offenders, and even, on occasion, knocked on their door – all to no avail. This is the point at which the local police are called to the complex. The consensus of the group after hearing all of the information presented is to have a team of mediators sent to the apartment complex to attempt to resolve the noise issue with the students. It is decided that the team will include a local police officer, campus security officer and the trained mediator from the university housing staff. It appears that the international students are from only one of the universities, so the team will be from that campus.

The housing staff mediator makes a call the next day to the student who owns the karaoke machine and arranges a session for the following week. The next task is to find all of the names and contact information for the other students involved in the noise complaints. This is done through the university rosters, as well as from the information gathered by the law enforcement agencies when they responded to the calls over the past few months. There are ten other students located and contacted to come to the mediation session at the complex the next week.

The day arrives for the mediation session and the parties arrive at the community room of the complex at 10am to mediate the noise issue. The mediators decide that with three of them, they will divide the parts of the session as follows: the housing mediator will take the lead by introducing all of the parties and making the opening statement. The campus security officer and the local police officer will each state the ground rules of the session (i.e. no interrupting, no foul language, no name calling and keeping the session confidential). The parties at the table (called disputants) each have a form in front of them to sign that agrees to the ground rules stated above. The session begins with the lead mediator asking for someone to begin the discussion of the noise complaints. Chang Le, the owner of the karaoke machine says that he would like to speak first. The mediator then asks the other parties at the table if they agree to this. They agree and Chang begins to speak. He says that they are in the middle of their Chinese New Year celebration which begins in early February and lasts for a few weeks. During this time he explains that one of the things they all like to do to celebrate is to play karaoke. He states that he proudly purchased the machine for the use of the entire group and that they really enjoy it. He explains to the mediators, "I have been a student here for four years and I will be graduating in May and getting a job as an engineer in the area. I love this town and would like to stay here. I even love this apartment complex and wish to remain here if these people would stop harassing me and my friends!"

The lead mediator thanks Chang for his statement and asks for someone from the other side to speak to the issues that have been raised. Monique, the French student asks to speak next. The mediator asks for group approval for her to speak, they all nod and Monique begins to give her side of the story. "You people have no idea how horrible this situation has become for the rest of us in the complex! These people have no regard for other people and their need for quiet time to study during the week. Forget about sleep – that hasn't happened for us for weeks! We call the police, call the campus security and housing staff, even the Dean of Students, and no one does anything about these rude people! We would move out, but the semester is half over and we have nowhere to go."

The mediator thanks Monique and begins to look for areas of Common Ground between the group. She begins by saying: "It seems that you are both saying that you want to continue living in the complex, but you have issues with the karaoke machine and the hours and length of time that it's played. Is there anyone who would like to speak to some issues of how to live together peacefully for the rest of the semester?"

A member of the Chinese group, Ying, agrees to speak and offers the following, "We love the karaoke! It is one of the only things that we can all enjoy together as a group, and I don't see why these people want to take that away. Who are they to make the rules?"

The campus security mediator interrupts, thanks Ying for her statement, and says, "The French students are simply stating their frustrations with the music issue and you are stating your frustrations with the complaints and not being able to listen to your music when you choose. Does anyone have any suggestions for a framework of rules that both sides come up with and that you can all live with until the end of the semester?"

The group decides that they would each like a few moments alone to discuss their options and then come back together to make suggestions. The mediators agree and lead one group to another room and keep the other group in the mediation room. They reconvene in about fifteen minutes with the following proposals: The Chinese students propose to continue with their karaoke, however, they offer to limit the activity to the weekends until midnight. The French students accept the proposal, stating that it would be more reasonable to have quieter hours during the week to study until the end of the semester. The mediators offer to put the agreement in writing. However, both sides must agree. The parties state that they would like the agreement in writing and that they would like the chance to discuss the new routine with the other side if conflict arises in the future. The parties agree to karaoke on the weekends only with a midnight cutoff time. They further agree that if issues involving noise and their living situations arise in the future, they will contact each other directly, rather than calling the police. The conclusion of the session sees both sides shaking hands and walking out with a copy of the written agreement. The mediators thank all parties for their positive participation in the mediation process. They also offer mediation to the parties, if future issues should arise.

Conflict Resolution and Disturbing the Peace

Disturbing the peace, and especially noise, is one of those areas where a law enforcement officer may require more conflict resolution skills than knowledge of the law. First of all, people who make noise are not always determined to commit a crime or break a local ordinance. Their intentions may be in having fun or practicing some form of celebration as seen in the case study. Secondly, without some form of conflict resolution skills, disturbing the peace calls have a high recidivism rate. In the case study, some type of law enforcement returned to resolve the dispute over twenty times. Sometimes what law enforcement may see as a violation may be perceived differently by the perpetrators.

Living in a democracy allows its citizens to have different points of view even when they are breaking an ordinance or a law (Marts, 1998). In this next section, we will look at some of the conflict resolution skills that may help in resolving disturbing the peace problems, especially when they pertain to noise.

Culture and Disturbing the Peace

For law enforcement officers, disturbing the peace and especially ordinances on noise, will find numerous gray areas when answering a call. In the case study, we see examples of this. First, the officer may need to realize that the people in dispute are looking at the conflict from different cultural perspectives. Without a certain understanding and knowledge of the cultures involved, an officer could make a decision based solely on local town ordinances regarding noise and miss the underlying cultural differences between the disputing parties. That is not to say that law enforcement should ignore ordinances or laws, but should realize more could be happening than enforcement of the law (Retzinger & Sheff, 2001). In the case study, each disputing party may have an investment in "not losing face" in front of people from another culture, or realize that certain rituals are being practiced that the other side does not completely understand (Barnes, 2006). This is not to say that law enforcement officers need to be sociologists but it may be important to understand the culture of the people within your jurisdiction. Here are some helpful issues to consider:

- Realize that losing face between people from different cultures is one of the biggest problems when people are in dispute and have little understanding of another culture's way of resolving conflict (Li & Merry, 1987).

- Realize that people from different cultures or backgrounds may not understand the issues involved in disturbing the peace disputes, especially noise, and may act emotionally rather than logically. This may require the law enforcement officers to understand certain emotions such as anger, resentment and revenge as viewed from each specific culture (Konstan & Chernoff, 2001).

- Realize that your jurisdiction may include numerous subcultures where each follows different rules of behavior. Consider the rules of the subculture while trying to uphold the noise ordinances or other actions that disturb the peace (Moore, 1996).

- Realize that other differences exist between groups of people beyond culture. For example, an eighteen-year-old male may view his music as soothing or exciting whereas an eighty-year-old male may only hear noise. Consider generational differences when dealing with disturbing the peace issues. Sometimes the "generation gap" plays a role in noise ordinances as much as the ordinance itself (Umbreit, 1997).

Mediation and Disturbing the Peace

For experienced mediators, the issue of disturbing the peace and especially noise, many times has gone on for much too long and other conflicts such as hatred and revenge have joined opposing parties when they come for mediation (Lancely, 2002). It may be that law enforcement officers can more directly deal with these types of disputes before what was considered a "pinch" between opposing parties has turned into a "crunch." The earlier issues, such as disturbing the peace are dealt with, the less baggage they bring to a judge or a mediator. Law enforcement officers are in position to mediate at the scene if they follow some basic skills in the mediation process. The following are skills that can be used when faced with opposing parties who feel one party is disturbing the peace:

Create Ground Rules — People from differing cultures and differing points of view have numerous cultural biases regarding the rituals and their right to enjoy themselves. In other words, they have their own preconceived set of ground rules. An effective law enforcement officer can quickly set up his or her own set of effective ground rules that when agreed upon, will cancel the cultural difference in the disputants. For example, if you can get opposing sides to follow these simple sets of rules, an issue of noise or other forms of disturbing the peace can be resolved:

- Have them agree that no foul language will be used during the mediation. This type of language is loaded with emotion that can derail mediation.

- Have an agreement that both sides will speak one at a time. This lowers the chances that the volume of one side will overpower the other.

- Make sure that both sides have an equal amount of time to speak. If one side does all of the talking, the other side may perceive the mediation as unfair.

- Make sure that both sides have an opportunity to vent their feelings (always under the guidelines agreed upon in the ground rules) before coming up with a plan to settle the dispute. Emotions of both sides may need to be expressed. In other words, do not move too quickly through the mediation process.

Anger Management and Disturbing the Peace

One thing is certain, that when a law enforcement officer answers a call for disturbing the peace, there probably will be one or more parties who have become angry. Disturbing the peace can be far more emotional than, for example, shoplifting in Chapter 3. It is similar to the experience of harassment in Chapter 1 or physical threats found in Chapter 2. When people get angry it is because they believe that a situation has become unreasonable, and noise and disturbing the peace have unreasonable behavior as one of the reasons for calling a law enforcement officer (Hankins, 1998). Keeping this in mind, it may help law enforcement officers to understand some of the guidelines used in conflict resolution pertaining to anger management. The following are a list of simple skills to consider when answering a disturbing the peace complaint.

Show Reasonable Behavior—Show reasonable behavior when talking to people who are in conflict over disturbing the peace. The climate surrounding these disputes is usually unreasonable and showing reasonable and objective behavior sets a different tone for the emotional climate of the dispute.

Use the Skill of Pacing—When stress builds it is possible to pace the disputants by breathing more slowly, and talking more slowly until the disputants calm down. As law enforcement officers and other persons of authority, most people in disturbing the peace cases will follow modeling behavior of the officer. Therefore, losing one's temper can have the opposite effect (Pilluta & Murnighan, 1996).

Help the Disputants Get Distance—Separating the disputants gives both sides an opportunity for reason to return and also an opportunity to slow the pace of the dispute. With the issue of noise, it may be important to stop the noise first before dealing with anyone. It becomes hard to be reasonable when an unreasonable act is taking place.

Help People Check Their Beliefs—This is especially true when it comes to noise issues between cultures. If both sides have not considered the beliefs of the opposing side, then anger is a likely possibility. Unchecked beliefs can cause unnecessary angry disputes. Also, make sure to represent the beliefs of the town ordinance against noise so that all beliefs from all parties are being considered.

Attack the Problem—When people explode with anger, have them attack the problem in your presence, not other people in the dispute. Sometimes trying to stop the explosions makes them worse. It may be wise to let the disputants vent their feelings only under the ground rules you have established and only towards the problem, not another person.

Get Closure — In the case study, the law enforcement officers had to come back numerous times because their warnings did not give closure to the dispute. It was only after both sides sat down and mediated a fair and equitable agreement that closure was obtained. Sometimes, only gathering facts in an angry dispute, makes the opposing parties believe you are acting as a judge, rather than a peace officer. Getting closure, changes that image from judge to referee and also helps in reducing the recidivism rate for these types of disputes.

Exercises

Responding to the Case Study (How would law enforcement officers respond to this disturbing the peace call from a *legal point of view?*)

Responding to the Case Study (How would law enforcement officers respond to this disturbing the peace call from a *conflict resolution point of view?*)

In the case study, how many options does law enforcement have from a legal point of view?

In the case study, if selecting a conflict resolution stance to the disturbing the peace call, law enforcement officers could use what skills?

How can ground rules help people who are disturbing the peace stop his or her behavior?

How would you show reasonable behavior in making a call for disturbing the peace?

What would you consider the most important mediation skills to use when answering a call for noise?

When would you suggest an arrest is in order for disturbing the peace?

Chapter 6

CRIMINAL MISCHIEF

Introduction

The intentional destruction of property is popularly referred to as vandalism. It includes behavior such as breaking windows, slashing tires, spray painting a wall with graffiti, and destroying a computer system through the use of a computer virus. Vandalism is a malicious act and may reflect personal ill will, although the perpetrators need not know their victim to commit vandalism. Criminal mischief in the form of vandalism has become a rather widespread phenomenon in modern society. It has been estimated that vandalism costs in the United States are far over a billion dollars (Sanders, 2005). For that matter, criminal mischief in general is on the rise especially in urban communities and schools (Pappalardo, 2002). However, vandalism is not only directed to the inner cities. Law enforcement officers may spend a considerable amount of their time investigating the willful damaging of property and the criminal mischief that accompanies this destruction.

The public's perception of vandalism and criminal mischief seems to focus its concerns surrounding the adolescent behavior of males in our society, yet older adults also participate in these criminal acts, usually for ideological motives. Nevertheless, some of the motivational factors for vandalism include peer group pressure, frustration aggression notions, mental instability and a desire for recognition and revenge (Whittingham, 1981).

Schools, subways, cemeteries, public parks, private homes and businesses all have been affected by the current wave of vandalism facing our law enforcement agencies in the 21st Century with the increase in the amount of graffiti spearheading the way. However, vandals do not necessarily vandalize based on impulsive behavior. Sometimes criminal mischief through the act of vandalism are intentional acts either to state one's frustrations or resentments or as a method for marking personal identity as found in gangs and other peer groups.

Furthermore, law enforcement may have to come to the conclusion that some adolescent vandals destroy property as an act of "play," making the response to criminal mischief in this area more complex and confusing. Sometimes reckless behavior is as much a motivation for vandalism as malicious destruction of or damage to the property of another. Therefore, people who vandalize others create a situation for law enforcement that may involve one or two people or an entire community, as in vandalizing a cemetery. For these reasons, law enforcement officers need to understand the options available to them so that repeated acts of vandalism do not persist.

Legal Criteria and Vandalism

Because the destruction of public and private property poses a threat to society, modern statutes make vandalism a crime. The penalties upon conviction may be a fine, a jail sentence, an order to pay for repairs or replacement, or all three. In addition, a person who commits vandalism may be sued in a civil tort action for damages so that the damaged property can be repaired or replaced.

Different Definitions of Vandalism

Vandalism is a general term that may not actually appear in criminal statutes. Frequently, these statutes employ the terms criminal mischief, malicious mischief, or malicious trespass as opposed to vandalism. A group of individuals can be convicted of conspiring or acting concertedly to commit vandalism. Generally, the attempt to commit vandalism is an offense as well, but the penalties for attempted vandalism are not as severe as the penalties for a completed act. Penalties also depend on the value of the property destroyed or the cost of repairing it (West's Encyclopedia of American Law, 2006).

Damage of Property

To obtain a conviction, the prosecution must ordinarily prove that the accused damaged or destroyed some property, that the property did not belong to the accused, and that the accused acted willfully and with malice. In the absence of proof of damage, the defendant may be guilty of trespass but not vandalism. If there is no proof that the defendant intentionally damaged the property, the defendant cannot be convicted of the crime but can be held liable for monetary damages in a civil action (Penal Law and Criminal Procedure Law of the State of New York, 2006).

Some state statutes impose more stringent penalties for the destruction of certain types of property. Such statutes might cover the desecration of a church or synagogue, the destruction of jail or prison property by inmates, and the intentional destruction of property belonging to a public utility.

Destructive acts will not be excused merely because the defendants acted out what they thought was a noble purpose. Political demonstrators may exercise their First Amendment rights of freedom of speech and assembly, but if they deface, for example, government property with spray-painted slogans, they can be convicted of vandalism (Ward, 1974).

Adolescence and Vandalism

The peak period for committing relatively minor property crimes is between the ages of fifteen and twenty-one. In the United States adolescent vandalism, including the wanton destruction of schools causes millions of dollars of damage each year. Apprehending vandals is often difficult, and the costs of repairing the damage are passed on to taxpayers, private property owners, and insurance companies. Some states hold parents financially responsible for vandalism committed by their minor children, up to specified limits. These statutes are designed to encourage parental supervision and to shift part of the cost of vandalism from the public to the individuals who are best able to supervise the children who destroyed the property.

In 1997, law enforcement agencies made approximately 136,500 arrests of persons under age 18 for vandalism. These juvenile arrests represented 44% of all vandalism arrests; males accounted for the majority (88%) of the juvenile arrests. Unlike most offenses, the racial distribution of youth arrested for vandalism in 1997 generally reflected their profile in the general population: white (80%), black (18%), American Indian (1%), and Asian (1%). The 1997 vandalism arrest rate peaked at age 16 and then declined for each subsequent age. Overall, the juvenile arrest rate for vandalism declined between 1980 and 1982 and then gradually increased to reach a high of 496 arrests per 100,000 youths, ages 10-17, in 1994. As with juvenile arrest rates overall, the juvenile arrest rate for vandalism declined between 1994 and 1997, and the 1997 rate was nearly the average of the prior 17 years (Stahl, 1997).

Types of Vandalism

The typical observer may think vandalism and break-ins are pointless, particularly when the offenders have focused on property destruction and have taken nothing of value. One can better understand the behavior when considering it in the context of adolescence, when peer influence is a particularly powerful motivator. Most delinquent acts are carried out by groups of youths, and vandalism is no exception. Participating in vandalism often helps a youth to maintain or enhance his or her status among peers. This status comes with little risk since, in contrast to playing a game or fighting, there are no winners or losers (Johnson 2005).

- **Peer-Influenced Vandalism** – Vandalism is committed to impress and obtain confirmation from peer groups.

- **Acquisitive Vandalism** – is committed to obtain property or money.

- **Tactical Vandalism** – is used to accomplish goals such as getting a community event or celebration cancelled.

- **Ideological Vandalism** – is oriented toward a social or political cause or message, such as a protest against community rules.

- **Vindictive Vandalism** – (such as setting fire to the principal's office after being punished) is done to get revenge.

- **Play Vandalism** – occurs when youths intentionally damage property during the course of play.

- **Malicious Vandalism** – is used to express rage or frustration. Because of its viciousness and apparent senselessness, people find this type particularly difficult to understand.

Case Study

Mike, Jim and Steve were all 16 years old and friends for as long as they could remember. They attended high school in the small town of 2,000 residents in the rural Midwest. The town was called Plainfield. It had a gas station, school, and market with a drug store. There wasn't much to do on a Friday night in the late Fall when football season was over and the dances at the school didn't start until after the holidays. The school year had been particularly difficult for them. Mike was failing most of his classes and, therefore, suspended from athletics until his grades improved. Jim's parents had just split up and Jim was living with his Dad until custody could be worked out during the divorce proceedings. Steve had just broken up with his girlfriend of two years, having been told that day in school that she never wanted to see him again. Needless to say, they weren't looking forward to the weekend.

The three friends met at the gas station at about 8 p.m. It had been dark since about 6 p.m. as it was mid-November. They sat at a booth having pizza slices and soda and discussing what to do that night. They decided to take a walk down the street past the cemetery and maybe get a six-pack and hide in the cemetery to drink. They went by Mike's house and took a couple of six-packs from the fridge and headed out. It was a cold and moonless November night. They came upon the cemetery where the gates were locked, so they jumped the fence and began to run. They settled in at the back of the cemetery and began to drink the beer. Halfway through the second six-pack, Mike showed his two friends a can of black spray paint that he had taken from his garage. He dared the other two to see how many of the headstones they could knock over or spray paint. The boys began to scatter in different directions with Mike taking the lead spraying headstones as he went. The other two began knocking over the headstones by forcefully kicking them. By the time the rampage was over, they had destroyed over twenty headstones in the cemetery. They saw flashlights coming their way and ran. They were pursued by the local police officer and told to stop where they were. Officer Jones grabbed Mike and the other two stopped. They were escorted to the police station and charged with criminal mischief (vandalism) and underage drinking. Officer Jones called their parents and they were given tickets with appearance dates in the local court for the coming week. The three boys appeared with their parents at the local court and went through the arraignment proceeding. Their cases were adjourned for two weeks to consult with attorneys and the district attorney. They each hired attorneys and met with them individually. The district attorney spoke with Officer Jones and asked for his recommendation as to the fate of the boys. Officer Jones pointed out that they were all 16 years old and therefore, eligible for Youthful Offender status as it was their first offense and they were between 16 and 19 years of age. He recommended that they participate in Victim Offender Mediation and that there was a local mediation center that provided the service. He said that he had success in the past with youthful offenders and victims meeting face to face. The district attorney agreed and approached the boys' attorneys with the offer of Youthful Offender status and Victim Offender Mediation. The attorneys met with the parties and the judge, who also recommended Victim Offender Mediation. The process was explained to the boys and their parents as a meeting to be set up between the boys and the cemetery association, who, in turn, would contact as many of the families as possible who wanted to meet with the boys to discuss the damages done to their loved one's headstones on that November night. It was carefully explained to the boys and their parents that the mediation could not take place if the association or the families did not agree to be at the meeting. Everyone agreed and the Victim Offender Mediation was set for the following Tuesday at 7 p.m. in the local courthouse.

The time came for the session and the following parties were escorted by the Victim Offender Mediator into the room: The defendants and their attorneys, the head of the cemetery association, and ten family members of the deceased whose headstones were damaged. The mediator sat at the head of the table with the cemetery association representative and family members on one side and the defendants and their attorneys on the other. The mediator began to explain the rules of the Victim Offender session: they would begin by making opening statements describing why they were at the session and what they hoped to accomplish from participating in the mediation. The mediator would keep track of equal time to speak, rules of courtesy (i.e. no interrupting, no foul language, no name calling, etc.), and, at the end, if appropriate and agreed upon by all of the parties, draft a Victim Offender Mediation Agreement. All parties agreed to devote two hours that evening to resolving the dispute. If more or less time was needed, it would be addressed and dealt with accordingly. Since there were only three defendants and eleven cemetery representatives, the mediator explained that in order to have equal time to speak they would have to balance each other's allotted time to speak.

The session began with agreement to all of the Ground Rules by the parties, and the cemetery association representative, Mr. Smith, speaking first:

"I have been involved with managing this association and dealing with families who have buried their loved ones in our town cemetery for nearly forty years. In that time I have never seen an incident as horrible as this one! I think these boys should pay for the damages that they have inflicted! I don't see how they will learn any other way."

The family members began to speak, one at a time. The first person, Mrs. Johnson, spoke of the sudden death of her husband three years ago and her struggle with depression since his death.

"I go to the cemetery every week that I can to visit Bob and talk about the things that have happened that week. When I went the other day, I was horrified to see black spray paint over his name on the headstone. I thought to myself, who could have done such a horrible thing."

The other family members spoke in turn about their shock and horror upon learning of the destruction of their loved one's headstones. Each person echoed the same sentiment: "How could someone have done such a horribly disrespectful thing?"

It was now time to hear from the boys who had been charged with the vandalism. They each spoke in turn, beginning with Mike.

"I feel the most responsible. It was my spray paint and I brought the beer. If we hadn't been drinking, we probably wouldn't have done it! We were just bored and frustrated with our lives and now look what we've caused!"

The other two boys spoke of their losses and disappointments that school year and how truly sorry they were for causing such pain to innocent families. They asked what they could do to make it right. It was now the cemetery rep's turn:

"Have you boys thought about paying for the damages by working at the cemetery to clean and repair any of the headstones, as well as working on the grounds with mowing, trimming and putting flags out for Memorial Day?"

The family members echoed their agreement with such a plan, as well as formal apologies from each boy to each family member involved. The boys agreed to work as long as they could until the weather made it impossible and to return in the Spring to continue working at the cemetery. The cemetery representative would also calculate the monetary damages to the headstones that could not be washed or repaired, and the boys would be responsible for paying the difference. Their work at the cemetery would be calculated at $8.00/hour and the difference would have to be made up out of their pockets.

All parties agreed and the mediator drew up the agreement to reflect the party's sentiments. The session ended with the boys making a formal apology to all present, and the families thanking them for having the courage to face them and admit to their wrong-doings. Each side was given a copy of the agreement. The boys appeared in court the following week and presented a copy of the agreement to the judge and the district attorney. The court accepted the agreement, but made it clear to the defendants that if they violated the agreement, they would be back in court to answer the original criminal mischief charges.

Conflict Resolution and Vandalism

Vandalism seems to be a phenomenon that continues to plague law enforcement agencies and communities at large. Obviously in more malicious cases of vandalism the courts and the justice system have a legal responsibility to control the spread of vandalism and for this reason many vandals may end up under arrest for the crimes they have committed. However, in the previous section on "Types of Vandalism" it becomes clear that not all vandals are motivated by malicious intent. This is especially true when we recognize the complex problems of identity and peer pressure that accompanies adolescence. For these reasons it may be important to the victims of vandalism and the vandals themselves, if some form of alternative dispute resolution is employed beyond being arrested for a crime. The following are two possible alternatives that may or may not be used in conjunction with being arrested for the crime of vandalism:

Victim Offender Mediation

Victim Offender Mediation is a face-to-face meeting in the presence of a neutral third party, between the victim of a crime and the person who committed the crime. The practice is also called victim-offender dialogue, victim-offender conferencing, victim-offender conciliation or restorative justice dialogue (Bazemore, Gordon & Schiff, 2001).

Victim Offender Mediation can have practical and successful resolution of disputes for law enforcement officers answering a call for vandalism. In the case study, more was accomplished by bringing the victims and the offenders together than simply arresting the vandals without any understanding of the damage they emotionally and psychologically had done to the victims of their crime.

Victim Offender Mediation and Law Enforcement — Law enforcement officers may find this form of conflict resolution valuable in vandalism cases if they have an understanding of what purpose it holds for the law enforcement officer, the victim, the offender and the community at large (Harrison, 2002). The following are reasons for considering using victim offender mediation when answering a call pertaining to vandalism or referring to the judge or district attorney some form of Victim Offender Mediation be used in certain cases:

- Victim Offender Mediation can neutralize differences in status and power and provide a climate where meaningful reconciliation can take place.

- The stories told by both victim and offender can be empowering to both parties.

- It allows law enforcement officers the option of mending hurtful feelings in a community by letting the victim and the offender confront each other in a mediation setting.

- Human beings possess inner resources that, under the right circumstances, can be accessed and used to address issues and resolve problems of importance.

- Discovering underlying needs and interests can enhance a collaborative effort and provide more satisfying results. The "personal" element is powerful: stories of individual experience can evoke empathy, insight, and understanding. Telling and hearing these stories can be empowering, validating, and transforming for both the speaker and the listener.

Guidelines for Victim Offender Mediation — The following guidelines are established by the Department of Justice and the Center for Restorative Justice and Peace Making (Umbreit, 2000):

- A fundamental guideline for Victim Offender Mediation programs is protecting the safety of the victim. The mediator must do everything possible to ensure that the victim will not be harmed.

- To ensure the safety of the victim, the mediation should be conducted in a location that the victim considers safe, and the victim should be encouraged to bring along a support person or two.

- Each mediation program should have its own criteria for case selection, such as type of offense, age of offender (juvenile or adult), first-time offense, or multiple offenses.

- A mediator usually meets first with the offender, prior to contacting the victim. Then, if the offender is willing to participate in mediation, the victim can be contacted and a meeting can be arranged (Coates, Kalani & Umbreit, 1994).

- The victim must always have the right to say "no" to mediation, to refuse to participate, and to have that decision honored and respected.

- The victim should have the opportunity to choose whether to speak first during the initial narrative portion of the mediation session or whether to speak last. This choice is given out of deference to his or her position as the victim of a crime – position the criminal and juvenile justice systems frequently ignore once the complaint has been filed (Bazemore, Gordon and Shiff, 2001).

- A victim has the right to select the restitution option that best meets his or her needs. In addition to reimbursement of out-of-pocket expenses, a victim may request that the offender undertake community service (a public service of the victim's choice), perform personal service for the victim, write a letter of apology, participate in treatment or other programs to improve his or her competence, or complete some other creative assignment. Although the final restitution plan will be negotiated with the offender, the victim must understand that he or she can request a particular compensation, within legal limits (Umbreit, Coates & Brown, 2004).

Peer Mediation and Vandalism

Schools have always been a major source for vandalism in our society. This is probably because adolescent behavior is more amenable to acts of vandalism than those of adults. A movement that recently has been taking place in public schools is to have a "Resource Officer" stationed at the school for safety, criminal behavior in the school, education and conflict resolution. Some of the most successful programs in using resource officers are in the area of peer mediation (Brinson, Fisher & Kottler, 2004). The following are reasons for law enforcement officers to consider peer mediation, whether you are stationed in a school as a "Resource Officer," or are called to a school for students who are vandalizing school property (Stomfay and Stitz, 1994):

- Conflict is a natural human state better approached with skills than avoidance.

- There are better ways to deal with conflict in schools than detention, expulsion, or court intervention.

- Mediation fosters a reduction in violence, vandalism and chronic absences.

- Mediation can improve communication and enhance the school climate.

- Mediation training helps both young people and teachers deepen their understanding about themselves and others and provides them with lifetime conflict resolution skills.

- Mediation training increases student interest in justice and the legal system while encouraging active citizenship.

- Shifting the responsibility for solving conflict from the adults to the youth frees teachers and administrators to concentrate on teaching.

- Recognizing the competence of young people enhances their self-worth, encourages growth and increases skills such as listening, critical thinking and problem solving.

- Mediation training assists in preparing students to live in a multi-cultural world.

- Mediation training provides a system of problem solving uniquely suited to the resolution of problems that youth might not take to parents or teachers.

Exercises

Responding to the Case Study (How would a law enforcement officer respond to this call from a *legal point of view?*)

Responding to the Case Study (How would a law enforcement officer respond to this call from a *conflict resolution point of view?*)

In the case study how many options does a law enforcement officer have from a legal point of view?

If selecting a conflict resolution stance to the vandalism call, a law enforcement officer could use what skills?

How can Victim Offender Mediation help a vandal stop his or her behavior?

How can Victim Offender Mediation help a victim reconcile his or her feelings?

What would you consider worthwhile community service for vandalism?

How could a Resource Officer in a school develop a peer mediation program?

Chapter 7

TRESPASS

Introduction

In an age of continued loss of privacy, trespass has become a more frequent issue for law enforcement, especially in countries where democracy is a way of life. In the United States, a person's right to own property is one of the fundamental rights found in the Constitution. Furthermore, people's right to privacy is constantly being debated, all under the umbrella of the Fourth Amendment in the United States Bill of Rights (Hefferman, 2001).

However, trespass in recent times has become more than unlawfully seeking access to another's property. For example, protesters may use trespass for political reasons or to draw attention to their message (Connelly, 2002). This can be seen in actions taken by protesters dealing with environmental issues, economic issues and social issues. In all of these, someone or a group of people willfully trespass in order to make some form of political statement. Activists may employ some form of civil disobedience in order to make their statement to a community or a society (Axelsen, 1995).

For law enforcement, entering someone else's private property or willfully breaking the law to make a political statement can be common occurrences that may require some form of legal action. Yet, in both of these incidences other forms of conflict resolution remedies can be used to help reduce the recidivism rate of frequent trespassers. Law enforcement officers acting as mediators or conciliators have resolved such disputes as long as no physical violence has taken place between the trespasser and the person or group who have had their rights violated under the law (Kuttner, 1999). However, this raises the issue of owning one's property and the rights that law enforcement may have to struggle with when others believe they have a right to trespass on other's private property.

Legal Criteria for Trespass

The criminal act of going on to somebody else's property without permission in some jurisdictions is an offense or misdemeanor while in other jurisdictions trespass is not considered a crime. In these circumstances, property is protected by civil law not penal law and the trespasser is not necessarily considered a criminal, as found in most criminal codes across the United States. Furthermore, not all seeking access to property, are trespassing. The law recognizes the rights of persons to give permission to invitees and persons who have the right to be on the property are called, licensees. For example, this group may include police officers, meter readers or process servers.

Making Your Property Private

Creating private property can be accomplished in a number of different ways. One of the most common methods for protecting your property against trespass is to erect signs that state, "Private Property" or "No Trespassing." However, other methods also can be used to insure your rights. Building a continuous fence accomplishes the same effect as the posting signs and marking your land with red paint on trees is also used in some jurisdictions (Mitchell, 1998). Also, some land owners may allow some trespassers while excluding others. This can be found on posted land that indicates that certain groups are not allowed on the property, yet others can enter it. For example, a sign that states, "No Hunting" could still allow others to cross the land without fear of any civil or criminal action.

The Use of Force and Trespass

Property owners in most jurisdictions can only use reasonable force to protect their property. The old myth that a person has the right to protect their property at all costs is in fact strictly a myth. For example, there are cases where the landowner set "booby traps" and was prosecuted for unreasonable use of force. Also, shooting at trespassers is, in most jurisdictions, strictly forbidden. However, in Texas you can use deadly force against trespassers after dark (Texas Penal Code: 9.42, 2006).

Removing Trespassers

In most jurisdictions property owners are not allowed to remove trespassers on their own. The usual procedure is to ask the trespassers to leave and if they refuse, to call law enforcement for their removal. Also, in most jurisdictions, as long as the trespasser is not causing an immediate threat, you cannot use bodily force to remove them. Furthermore, property owners cannot detain or make a citizen's arrest because this will not allow the trespasser to make the decision to leave voluntarily. However, there is the experience of "Benevolent Trespassing" where, for example, there is an automobile accident and someone needs to enter the property to call for help or to ask for help. In these cases common sense would indicate that any form of removal by physical force would be unacceptable. This also includes emergencies where damage to the property may occur. In these cases, property damage would not fall under the guidelines of trespass when the life of another is in danger. Doctors and EMT workers may need different standards than common trespass in order to save a life or reach somebody who is in imminent harm (Anderson, 2004).

Police Trespassing

Law enforcement officers regularly walk and drive onto private property. It happens so often it's hardly noteworthy. Although some might call it "trespassing," to most people it's insignificant, a nonevent. Sometimes, however, it does become important when officers see something that results in a search or an arrest. However, evidence discovered as the result of an entry onto private property will be suppressed if the officers' entry constituted an illegal "search." Yet, officers routinely commit technical or "common law" trespassing which is the act of walking or driving onto private property without the owner's permission. For the most part, this is a common practice and is not considered a crime, except when it leads to an unlawful search. In numerous calls, police may practice technical trespass as a routine method of keeping a community safe. The intentions of the law enforcement officers are not to trespass but to act out his or her duties in the protection of the community (Cutting, 2001).

Case Study

The Richards and Gonzalez families had been neighbors in the city of Grandy for nearly fifteen years. Their children had attended school together and played sports, as well as being neighborhood friends. The neighborhood picnic on July 4th each year was an event that was happily anticipated by all. The summer was only a couple of weeks old, yet it was already unseasonably warm. The neighborhood kids had already started running through the local fire hydrants and waiting for the weekends to head to the beaches. The neighbors started to plan for the July 4th picnic, which was to be held at the Richards' house this year. Everyone pitched in by donating paper plates, cups, ice, drinks and one main dish to share. The grill was always going and one of the neighbors would volunteer to do the barbeque. Everyone seemed to be getting along well on Center Street that summer. The calls had all been made to invite the neighbors to the Richards for the annual picnic.

It was a couple of days before the picnic and the Richards were busy mowing their tiny yard and planting flowers, painting and cleaning up their yard. The Gonzalez family, their next door neighbors, were helping with the preparations. The Gonzalez family had a dog named Pepper, who was in the habit of running into the Richards yard. This usually wasn't a problem. However, on this day, the dog ran through the yard digging up dirt and all of the newly planted flowers with it. Bill Richards began yelling at Pepper, which prompted the Gonzalez daughter, Maria, age 10, to go over to the neighbors to see what all of the yelling was about. Bill Richards began yelling at her, "You had better get out of my yard and take that damn dog with you! We have worked so hard on this lawn and now it is ruined!" At this point, Maria began to cry and, through her tears, apologized to Bill Richards and ran home carrying Pepper.

Maria ran into her house crying and screaming, "Mr. Richards just yelled and swore at me and told me to take Pepper and never set foot in his yard again—none of us!" Anna, Maria's mother, came into the kitchen to comfort her daughter and see what had happened next door.

She asked her daughter, "What happened next door? Are you hurt? Is Pepper hurt?"

Maria replied, "No, mama, I'm just upset because Mr. Richards yelled at me!"

The entire family was now coming into the kitchen to see what had happened, led by Maria's father, Hector Gonzalez. He began to question her about the actions of his neighbor. Maria again explained, through her sobbing, what had happened.

"I'm going over there right now and straighten this out!" Hector stated. "You all stay here and keep that dog in the house!"

Hector stormed through the yard and knocked on his neighbor's back door. He pounded so loudly that it seemed as though he might break the door down! "I know you're in there, Bill, come out and face me, or do you just like to scare little girls! I want you to face me and tell me what you said to my daughter that upset her so much. I'm waiting here until you come out."

Bill Richards came to the back door and yelled, "Listen, Hector, if you don't leave my yard right now, I'm calling the police. You need to calm down and go home!"

"I will not," Hector replied, "until you come out here and face me!"

Bill Richards picked up the phone and dialed 911. "Hello, this is Bill Richards at 16 Center Street. I'd like to report a trespass. My neighbor, Hector Gonzalez, is outside my back door yelling and screaming at me and my family. I asked him to leave and warned him that if he didn't, I'd call the police. I want you to send an officer over here right now!"

The dispatcher tried to calm Mr. Richards down and ask some more questions before sending an officer to the scene. "Mr. Richards, has there been any physical violence?"

"No, ma'am, just shouting and foul language, but there could be some violence if he doesn't shut up and leave!"

"Ok, Mr. Richards, we'll send someone right over. Please wait where you are until the officer arrives," the dispatcher said.

It was about twenty minutes later when the neighbors saw the patrol car pull up in front of 16 Center Street. Officer James went to the front door and rang the bell. Bill Richards came to the door and ushered Officer James into the house.

"I'm so glad you came so quickly, I was afraid of what he would do!"

"Is there a place where we can sit down so that I can take your statement, Mr. Richards?"

"Yes, of course, Officer, right this way."

He led Officer James to the kitchen. They sat at the table and the officer took out his note pad and began to ask for information regarding the incident. Mr. Richards gave his side of the story as follows:

"I was over in my back yard mowing, planting flowers and cleaning up for the annual neighborhood 4th of July picnic when, suddenly, that damn dog from next door runs into our yard and begins running in circles and digging up all of the flowers that I had just spent hours planting! I began yelling at the dog, at which point the Gonzalez girl, Maria, comes running over, picks up the dog, and runs home. Next thing I know, her father, Hector, is banging at my back door, cursing and threatening to beat me up if I don't come outside and tell him what happened. At that point, I warned him that I was calling 911 if he didn't leave my yard. He ignored me, and that's when I called you!"

"Now, Mr. Richards, are you sure he threatened you with assault?"

"Absolutely," Bill replied. "If you hadn't come so quickly, who knows what might have happened!"

"I think I have enough information from you, Mr. Richards. Were there any witnesses to these actions?"

"I don't know if anyone actually saw it, but they sure heard it!"

"Thank you Mr. Richards" Officer James replied. "I'd like to talk to you about mediating this dispute between you and your neighbor. I would like to go next door and talk to him and his daughter and see if he would be agreeable to coming over here to speak with you and I will act as the mediator. This means that I won't take sides and I won't judge either one of you, but I will try to get you to talk to each other without shouting or name calling. Would it be alright with you if I went next door now?"

"I guess that would be okay with me," Bill replied.

Officer James went next door and knocked on the Gonzalez's door. Hector answered the door. "Am I glad you're here—that neighbor of mine is crazy—he tried to assault my daughter because of our dog being in his yard!"

"Is there a place that we can sit down and talk, Mr. Gonzalez, and maybe speak with your daughter about this incident?"

"Yes, officer, please come in." He led Officer James to the kitchen where they sat at the table.

Officer James began, "I have heard your neighbor's side of this dispute, and, now, I would like to hear yours."

"Okay, this guy is nuts! We've been neighbors for years and never had any problems. Today he loses it over my little dog, Pepper, and takes it out on my daughter who is only 10 years old! I would like to charge him with harassment! Am I under arrest for anything?"

Officer James replied, "No one is under arrest, Mr. Gonzalez. I would like to propose that you come next door with me and mediate this dispute with Mr. Richards. I will act as the mediator. There will be ground rules, such as no name calling, no foul language and no interrupting each other. If you settle the dispute, I can write up the agreement and you'll both get a copy. How does that sound to you?"

"I guess I could go over with you, as long as you keep him under control!"

Officer James and Mr. Gonzalez walked next door and knocked on the Richards door. Bill Richards answered the door and invited the men in. He escorted them to the kitchen table. Officer James sat at the head of the table and began the mediation as follows:

"Since you both have agreed to mediate, I am going to ask you, one at a time, to agree to these ground rules before we begin:

(1) No name calling. Can you both agree?"

Both men say "yes."

"(2) No foul language. Can you agree?"

Both men say "yes."

"(3) No interrupting. Can you both agree?"

Both men say "yes."

"Now, who would like to begin?"

"I would." Mr. Richards replies.

"Is that okay with you, Mr. Gonzalez?"

Mr. Gonzalez replies, "yes."

Mr. Richards gives his side of the story and Mr. Gonzalez listens. They establish that they were getting ready for the picnic when the dog ran into the yard and tore up the flowers. Mr. Richards acknowledged that he should not have yelled at Maria and he apologized. Mr. Gonzalez accepted the apology and stated that he would come over with his wife and daughter and replant the flowers and help get ready for the picnic. Both sides acknowledged that things got out of hand and they still wanted to be friends. The men shook hands and Officer James thanked them for being able to resolve their dispute without formal charges. He said goodbye, got into his patrol car and left. The two families began repairing the lawn. It was a beautiful 4th of July holiday that followed. Both families were talking to each other and no further problems developed.

Conflict Resolution and Trespass

Trespass is a law enforcement issue that may be better served by some form of mediation. In the above case study, Officer James realizes that quick action can help these neighbors avoid some of the escalating problems that start with accusations of trespass only to turn into more criminally acute problems, such as assault.

One of the quickest and most effective methods for resolving disputes that were displayed in the above case study, can be through some form of on-site community mediation. The following are the steps needed in order to successfully mediate a dispute when trespass is involved.

What is Mediation?

The following points help to describe a common community mediation process that can be used by law enforcement officers when confronted with calls concerning minor trespass disputes (Ladd, 2005):

- Mediators help disputing parties hear both sides of a dispute so they can make their own judgments

- Mediators listen for issues and emotions that clarify both parties' points of view.

- In mediation those in dispute are responsible for resolving the dispute. The law enforcement officer acts as a neutral third party.

- Final agreements in mediation are made by the parties in dispute.

- Mediation is one more conflict resolution skill that law enforcement officers believe that an arrest may actually make matters worse.

Steps of Mediation

The following are steps that law enforcement officers can use in order to mediate disputes such as trespass and other minor offenses. These steps can be accomplished by referring disputants to a community mediation service or, as demonstrated in the case study, can be used by the policeman when answering a call. In the case study, referring the two neighboring families to a mediation service may have been too late. On-site mediation can be effective especially when the dispute appears that it will become more serious for both sides to wait for any given period of time. For officer James it required some basic skills to mediate a fair and balanced agreement between the Gonzalez and Richards families. The following are five steps to mediation to consider when mediating a dispute:

Step 1: Creating a Climate of Neutrality — In creating a climate of neutrality it is important to establish a neutral setting from the beginning (Mayer, 2003). In the case study, Officer James first took the statement of Mr. Richards and got an agreement to mediate before he approached Mr. Gonzalez. He was now in a position to offer Mr. Gonzalez the opportunity to join Mr. Richards in resolving the dispute. By both parties agreeing to mediate from the beginning Officer James has created a sense of balance and he has accomplished this by remaining neutral. In successful mediation by law enforcement officers equality, neutrality and balance must be upheld or people in dispute may not openly express their thoughts and feelings (Winslade, 2000). Officer James, Mr. Richards and Mr. Gonzalez created a workable climate where thoughts and feelings were expressed and the mediation process continued in a fair and equitable manner (Slaikue, 1985).

Step 2: Finding Common Ground — For law enforcement officers this next step may be quite different than other training that they have received. For the most part, law enforcement is concerned with differences. For example, looking for differences in both parties, explanation of what happened or looking for differences that would indicate that someone is breaking the law. In the case study, Officer

James started out his investigations by looking for differences. It was only when he realized that neither side had committed assault or had caused any bodily injury that he turned to the mediation process. He realized that in order to stop a more serious crime from being committed, he now should begin to look for what these two families had in common (Moore, 2003). Finding common ground is probably the strongest tool that Officer James can use to bring these families back together. The more common ground established the less chance they will take their differences out on each other (Lang & Taylor,2000). Here are some of the common ground issues that Officer James can point out to Mr. Richards and Mr. Gonzalez:

- You both agree that you have been friendly neighbors for many years.

- You both agree that Pepper has entered Mr. Richards' yard in the past and has not caused any problems.

- You both agree that this was a one-time event and does not reflect the nature of your friendship.

- You both agree both sides got a little out of hand and lost their tempers.

- You both agree that neither of you wants to wreck the 4th of July celebration.

With all of this common ground agreement the chances of this escalating into an assault are minimized and the chance of this becoming a recurring problem are also minimized.

Step 3: Isolating Issues—From establishment of all the common ground what remains becomes the issues of the dispute. For example, in the case study, the two biggest issues were their friendship and the issue of both losing their tempers. Also, the issue of Anne becoming afraid may need discussion. Isolating issues in a community, mediation can be quite different than isolating issues in a court of law (Bennet & Herman, 1997). In a court of law, the lawyers are looking for those issues that will win their case. In a mediation , the issues that are important are those issues left over after you have established enough common ground (Ross,1997). Officer James may have said to them after establishing common ground, "Ok, Mr. Richards and Mr. Gonzalez, what issues do we still need to talk about?" The officer does not analyze the issues but merely asks what else needs to be discussed.

Step 4: Choosing Options—Choosing options can be an important stage for bringing people in dispute back together. A law enforcement officer can empower both parties to work out a remedy on their own and, in that way, they have ownership of the agreement (Goodman,1996). At this stage of the mediation process, the law enforcement officer acts as a referee in the bargaining between the two people in dispute. The law enforcement officer can help the disputing parties in minor ways such as: reminding them of previously isolated issues, pointing out any new issues that may need discussion and by presenting one party's option to the other side in an understandable and reasonable manner.

Making an Agreement—After options are negotiated, the law enforcement officer can encourage both side to make an agreement that is fair and reasonable. For example, in the mediation between Mr. Richards and Mr. Gonzalez, an agreement was made to help each replant the flowers and get ready for the 4th of July celebration. In the final step in mediation, the mediator helps develop a plan based on the wishes of both people in dispute. Here are some pointers in how to make sure the agreement is effective (Ladd, 2005):

- Make sure that the agreement is complete. Do not assume that everything is included in the agreement until you ask both sides whether they are comfortable with it.

- It is important that the agreement be specific. The more specific the agreement the better chance it will last. Vague agreements sometimes have a shorter life span.

- Make sure that the agreement is balanced. If Mr. Richards gets everything and Mr. Gonzalez gets nothing, then the agreement is in jeopardy of being followed.

- Use the language of the disputing parties in the agreement. It is their agreement and police language or legal language will only confuse what both parties have agreed to.

Exercises

Responding to the Case Study (How would Officer James respond to this call from a *legal point of view?*)

Responding to the Case Study (How would Officer James respond to this call from a *conflict resolution point of view?*)

In the case study, what other types of common ground could Officer James point out to the neighbors?

What other issues do you think were important in the case study?

What would be your particular style in helping disputants create options to resolve their dispute?

What do think would have been a fair and balanced
agreement between Mr. Richards and Mr. Gonzalez?

Try drawing up the agreement between Mr. Richards and Mr.
Gonzalez. Remember to be specific, balanced and in their
own words.

Chapter 8

DOMESTIC VIOLENCE

Introduction

Some estimates say that almost one million incidents occur against a current or former significant other per year (Bureau of Justice, 2003). One in five female high school students reports being physically and/or sexually abused by a dating partner. Abused girls are significantly more likely to get involved in other risky behaviors. They are 4 to 6 times more likely to get pregnant and 8 to 9 times more likely to have tried to commit suicide (Silverman, Raj & Clements, 2004). 1 in 3 teens report knowing a friend or peer who has been hit, punched, slapped, choked or physically hurt by his/her partner (Claiborne, 2005). For law enforcement agencies, domestic violence has become a major problem and it is growing. 92% of women say that reducing domestic violence and sexual assault should be at the top of any formal efforts taken on behalf of women today (Center for the Advancement of Women, 2003).

For law enforcement officers, domestic violence is a constant problem anytime an officer answers a call in a family dispute. However, one of the problems facing law enforcement is that there are circumstances where the abused partner will not press charges because of fear, low self-esteem, feelings of helplessness, shame, depression and social withdrawal (Miller, Cohen & Wiersema, 1996).

However, domestic violence is really about power and control. The abuser wants to dominate the victim/survivor and wants all of the power in the relationship – and uses violence in order to establish and maintain authority and power. Perpetrators of domestic violence are usually not sick or deranged, but have learned abusive, manipulative techniques and behaviors that allow them to dominate and control others and obtain the responses they desire (Dutton, 1998). While the public may think of domestic violence abusers as out of control, crazy, and unpredictable, the contrary is most often true. Use of psychological, emotional, and physical abuse intermingled with periods of respite, love, and happiness are deliberate coercive tools used to generate submission. Abusers may violently assault and within minutes offer words of regret. Many will buy gifts of flowers, candy and other presents in order to win favor and forgiveness. This creates a very confusing environment for victims. Abusers may say they will never harm their partners again, and promise to obtain help or counseling. Often, these promises are only made to prevent victims from leaving. Without getting help, the violence will most likely recur (Bergen, 1998).

Legal Criteria for Domestic Violence

The following constitutes legal criteria for domestic violence. In this case, we are using New Jersey's domestic violence guidelines. Different States in the U.S. have similar criteria; however, the terminology may differ according to each State. Victims of domestic violence means, a person who is 18 years of age or older or an emancipated minor who have been subjected to domestic violence by (N.J.S.A. 2C:25-19, 2006):

- A spouse or former spouse.

- Any other person who is a present or former household member.

- Any person whom the victim has had a dating relationship.

- Any person who anticipates having a child in common.

Making an Arrest

In many States there are certain conditions that exist where law enforcement officers must make an arrest regardless of the desires of the victims. An officer must make an arrest and sign a criminal complaint against a domestic violence defendant when:

- There are signs of physical injury.

- When there is a warrant in effect.

- When an order of protection was violated.

- When a weapon was used in the domestic violence dispute.

Discretionary Arrest—A law enforcement officer may make an arrest or may sign a criminal complaint against a person if there is probable cause and none of the above criteria apply. In these cases, the officer should inform the victim that he or she could sign a complaint. If the victim signs the complaint, the officer should make an arrest and take the suspect into custody (N.J.S.A. 2C: 25-21cb, 2006).

Discretionary arrests can take place when both parties are injured and the following factors should be used to determine which of the two should be arrested as the domestic violence assailant:

- Comparing the extent of the injuries suffered.

- The history of domestic violence between the parties.

- Each person's fear of physical harm, if any, which resulted from the other person's threatened or actual use of force.

- Whether a person was acting in self-defense and inflicted injury on the aggressor.

Obtaining a Temporary Restraining Order

If the victim qualifies for a Temporary Restraining Order and requests an immediate court order, the officer shall contact the designated judge by telephone, radio, or other means of electronic communication. The officer should:

- Assist the victim in preparing a statement which the victim will make to the judge.

- Explain to the victim that the judge will place him or her under oath and will ask questions about the incident.

- The victim will complete the domestic violence complaint.

- Have the victim sign the domestic violence complaint.

- The officer will then be instructed to serve the restraining order upon the alleged offender (N.J.S.A. 2C:25-28, 2006).

These points are just some of the legal criteria that must be considered by law enforcement when domestic violence has become an issue when answering a call. The following is an example of a typical domestic violence case study where the victim is afraid to press charges.

Case Study

George and Mindy were well known to the local law enforcement personnel. They had a history of domestic violence and both had been arrested for the offense. George said when he was arrested that he was trying to defend himself against Mindy's physical attacks and when he gave her a black eye, it was reason enough for the responding law enforcement officer to arrest George for physical abuse. However, Mindy was not necessarily the victim all of the time. She was bigger than George and she grew up in a household where violence was commonplace. Mindy was arrested after George's arrest when she put him in the hospital with a broken arm and leg. She had taken a frying pan and chased George until her aim was exact for doing the most damage.

Law enforcement and the Courts tried everything from arrest to a temporary restraining order to try and solve the problem. However, they were well-known in the community and it was not very long until they found a way to get back together. Adding to this, both of them would not sign a complaint when the officer on call knew that they had been violent yet could not find any physical evidence to make an arrest. Somehow, they were just as antagonistic against law enforcement as they were against each other. They had a reputation for having a chronic problem, but they always stopped short of being sentenced to prison time.

One evening Officer Dan received a call to investigate a domestic violence complaint at 42 Elm Street. He immediately knew what this meant. George and Mindy were at it again and he wondered just how far they had gone this time. When he arrived, they both admitted pushing each other around, but would not admit to any forms of physical violence. In the past it was Officer Dan who had arrested both of them, so he already knew that getting either of them to file a complaint was out of the question. Plus, he was convinced that arresting one of them only would make matters worse. Instead, he decided to try and reconcile the conflict between them.

First he asked them if they could remember how these fights would begin. After some discussion, it turned out that it seemed to be over some form of jealous feelings that both of them would dwell on after men and women would flirt with them at the local corner bar. By the time they got back to their duplex on Elm St., they were both fired up for some form of physical violence. Officer Dan then asked them, "What do you think triggers all of this rage?" Both George and Mindy knew immediately. It was the flirting that took place when they would drink and socialize around other people. He also asked them, "What is going on in your minds when you see another person flirting with your spouse?" After thinking for a while they admitted that it made them look bad in front of other people and they both agreed that the other people influenced their flirting. Officer Dan then asked them, "Do you really want to be with other people or are you jealous of the attention the other is getting?" Neither would admit to that, but Officer Dan said that:

> *Your jealous behavior seems to get out of hand to the point that violence begins. It is hard for me to believe you enjoy the restraining orders and the arrests simply because you are afraid of losing each other to someone else. Plus, I do not think the drinking has helped you with your decision-making abilities. Maybe we can sit down and come up with a list of rules to help you stop this problem.*

George, Mindy and Officer Dan sat down for about fifteen minutes and came up with a set of rules that they would try to fulfill when they felt jealous urges coming over them. Here is the list that George and Mindy created:

- Remind each other that the warning signal that sets off their violent behavior is usually around jealousy in the form of flirting. Each time they go to socialize they will agree to remind each other of the warning signal.

- Tell each other beforehand that they are beginning to feel jealous so that something can be done before it simmers and turns into violence when they get home.

- Do not embarrass the other person when someone is flirting. Simply, ask if you can talk to each other in private and avoid judging each other.

- If none of that works, have a rule before you use force that one of you will leave to get some distance until you have both calmed down.

- Let each other know when it is over and make up.

From that time on, George and Mindy tried to live by these ground rules. Sometimes they broke one or two of them but they were able to not break all of them. Officer Dan had empowered them to do what the courts had failed to do. He had given them a reason for not fighting.

Conflict Resolution and Domestic Violence

First of all, there are two other avenues open for cases where domestic violence is prevalent among people who know each other. First, we have reviewed some of the legal procedures that can be enforced when domestic violence is found. In many of these cases, the violence will determine the direction taken. In more severe cases, an arrest may be mandatory under the law of that State. Secondly, there are numerous advocate organizations that law enforcement officers can make referrals for victims of domestic violence. Some of these are:

- National Coalition Against Domestic Violence

- National Domestic Violence Hotline

- American Forces Information Services – Domestic Violence

- Family Violence Prevention Fund

- Domestic Violence Awareness Handbooks

- Domestic violence and sexual assault legislation in Congress

Beyond these resources, there are local "Women's Shelters" with counseling and education for those who have become victims of domestic violence. Shelters often offer temporary as well as transitional living programs, where women and their children can live in an agency-owned apartment for an extended period of time, during which they receive counseling and assistance. To be accepted into a program, women are interviewed and must demonstrate need. The cost is usually on a sliding scale, dependent on a woman's ability to pay. There is usually a waiting list for transitional living apartments because it is a much-needed service. Beyond the use of shelters, there are also excellent books on the topic such as, Domestic Violence Survival Guide and other notable books (Mariani & Sokolich, 1996).

However, in limited cases, there are times when a law enforcement officer can see an opportunity to help couples with their behavior. In the case study, it probably would not have made much difference to arrest either George or Mindy, one more time. Mindy could have gone to a women's shelter but neither George nor Mindy really wanted to be apart from each other. And, even though social services agencies deal with many cases regarding domestic violence, they are not always at the scene of the dispute, sometimes for days or weeks. In such cases of domestic violence that does not require an arrest, a law enforcement officer may want to attempt some form of reconciliation with the couple. The following skills may help law enforcement when answering a domestic violence call.

Emotions and Domestic Violence

Two emotional problems that are most commonly associated with domestic violence are found in the emotions of jealousy and revenge (Ladd, 2005). In both of these emotions, violence is usually not impulsive but is thought out and seems justified in the mind of the assailant. In this section, we will take you through the stages of jealousy and revenge for those limited cases where the opportunity lends itself to reconciliation. As law enforcement officers, you may have the opportunity to stop violence before it begins.

Jealousy and Domestic Violence—Jealousy may be at the root of many domestic violence cases. It is when one partner feels afraid of losing something from the other partner. In the case study, George and Mindy were afraid of losing their partner to another man or woman. However, there are other areas where being afraid of losing something can justify domestic violence in the minds of assailants (Holtz-Munroe, Stuart & Hutchinson, 1997). The following also should be considered potential areas of loss when considering a domestic violence cases (Ladd, 2005):

- *Afraid of Losing Face* can be seen in the case study. Neither, George nor Mindy wanted to be embarrassed in front of others. Their conclusions of possible embarrassment eventually led them to violence. This is a common problem with a dysfunctional couple with low self esteem. Any threat to their identity could cause a violent reaction (Yau-Fai Ho, 2004).

- *Afraid of Losing "Turf"* is another domestic violence issue. Couples in these situations sometimes look at their partner as an object not a person. In their minds they may see that person as a part of their "turf" and feel justified in some violent act to regain their turf.

- *Afraid of Losing Power and Control* becomes a major issue in some domestic violence cases. The whole act of domestic violence is perceived by the assailant through the themes of power and control. Beyond any love, jealous people value power and control far more than intimacy or affection.

Domestic Violence Skills (Jealousy) — There are certain skills that law enforcement officers can practice if the rare opportunity presents itself to conciliate a domestic violence dispute. The following skills could be effective in these cases:

- Knowing the *Warning Signals* that lead to domestic violence can reduce the use of it. In the case study Officer Dan points out to George and Mindy that the "flirting" is a warning signal that action must be taken to ward off the potential for domestic violence. They devise a plan where justification for violence is addressed when they notice flirting happening to either party.

- Finding *Common Ground* can be a deterrent to potential domestic violence. The more common ground established the less perceived differences between the couple. In the case study, Office Dan reminds them that both know that arrests have not worked and they agree they want to remain together.

- Explaining the *Logic Behind Using Force* may be another method for reducing domestic violence. In the case study, Officer Dan points out that the restraining orders have not worked and the drinking actually causes more violence. In effect, he says to them that drinking and flirting do not mix and to be cautious when involved in both behaviors. However, he goes beyond lecturing and helps them develop a logical plan of action when such behaviors collide.

Revenge and Domestic Violence — Revenge may be another cause of couples engaged in domestic violence. The act of revenge begins when one party feel violated by the other. In the case study, George and Mindy felt violated when either of them is found flirting with others and they decide to get even. Again, they have an excuse for eventual violence when they return to their duplex. Revenge seems to be justified in the minds of people who feel violated. At some point, they consciously or unconsciously decide to get even and eventually retaliate. Again we see that domestic violence is not caused by impulsive "crazy people." It can be a premeditated act based on a previous violation by their partner (Smedes, 1985). The following are some of the justifications people who practice domestic violence may make before committing a violent act:

- Many domestic violence assailants believe they have a *Right to Get Even* and explaining they have no right to get even rarely has any impact on them (Sheff,1997). These individuals start by feeling violated and emotionally thrown out of balance. In the case study, both George and Mindy justified their right to get even when the other party broke the unspoken rule concerning flirting. When either of them flirted, they decided a rule of the relationship was broken and action must be taken.

- Many domestic violence assailants come up with a plan of action that includes some form of violent retaliation. In effect, they come up with a plan of action based on revenge. In the case study, Officer Dan helps them to come up with a *Plan of Action Based on Justice* – not revenge – when he conciliates their problem by giving them five steps to stop their behavior. Usually, if a plan of justice is not introduced into a domestic violence dispute the assailant has a high probability of repeating the offense (Volkan, 1998).

Domestic Violence Skills (Revenge) — There are certain skills that a law enforcement officer may want to consider when involved in a case concerning domestic violence and revenge:

- Helping the couple *Create Boundaries* may help them construct limits to people's behavior. In the case study, Officer Dan creates boundaries by giving them a plan to overcome the flirting issue in their relationship. Sometimes couples do not know the boundaries of their partnership and may step over them, causing the other to feel violated. This was what happened in the case study. Neither of them understood the boundaries of their relationship and that flirting and possibly drinking and flirting would lead to domestic violence.

- It may be important to explain that *Revenge is a Problem, not a Solution to a Problem* (Retzinger, 1996). Many couples in domestic violence cases use revenge as a solution to a problem of feeling violated in some way by their partner. In this manner, they can justify their behavior. Revenge is a serious problem in domestic violence cases; it allows the assailant to feel a "justification" for his or her actions. The more law enforcement can help physical abusers to understand that they have a problem and not a solution to a problem, the better chance of them not repeating the offense.

Exercises

Responding to the Case Study (How would Officer Dan respond to this call from a *legal point of view?*)

Responding to the Case Study (How would Officer Dan respond to this call from a *conflict resolution point of view?*)

In the case study, what other types of common ground could Officer Dan point out to George and Mindy?

What other issues do you think were important in the case study?

Can you see any other times that conflict resolution could be used in a domestic violence case?

What do you think would be appropriate follow-up to Officer Dan's conciliation with George and Mindy?

What would be your next plan of action if conflict resolution did not work?

Should an arrest or filing a complaint be used most of the time? Explain why Yes or No.

Chapter 9

PARENTAL RESPONSIBILITY (ADOLESCENCE)

Introduction

F or law enforcement officers, the issue of parental responsibility has become a major problem, especially with adolescent criminal behavior. Answering a call where parents and adolescents are in conflict can bring up the topic of making decisions about parental responsibility. For parents, their responsibility is to make sure their children are safe from such problems as physical, sexual and emotional abuse in addition to supplying basic needs such as, shelter, self-esteem, morals, values, discipline and a child's education. (Thiesen, 2004). For parents, problems in these areas have created various types of legislation mandating a minimum level of parental responsibility. The objective of these laws is to impose affirmative duties on parents to provide necessities for the youth in their custody and to ensure they do not abuse or abandon their children. Other related efforts to establish a minimum standard of parenting include compulsory school attendance laws and criminal nonsupport laws (Davison, 1996).

However, such legislation can be vague and may infringe upon family privacy making the job of law enforcement more difficult when finding the line between the privacy of parents and parental responsibility for crimes committed by the adolescent behavior of their children. The sponsors of these laws argue that parental delinquency is usually the cause of the juvenile delinquency, but opponents argue that there is little evidence to support the claim that youth crime is caused by "bad parenting" and that there are many other social, cultural and economic causes that should be addressed, as more parents are forced to work long hours and hold two or more jobs to earn enough to cover basic family needs (Yee, 1999).

Considering all of the factors facing law enforcement regarding parent responsibility, keeping a balance between legal action and conflict resolution may be a consideration when an officer responds to a call that includes parental responsibility.

Legal Criteria for Parental Responsibility

There is a movement for greater parental accountability following a number of highly publicized violent crimes committed by children. While all States allow parents to be sued for the various actions of their children, the idea of criminal legislation to enable the prosecution of adults for "neglectful" parenting is relatively new. For example, a number of states have enacted or proposed laws that will automatically hold parents financially responsible for all expenses associated with a second false bomb threat or 911 call made by a child and could impose a prison term of up to 18 months and order payment of restitution to any victims if the child commits a serious crime (Pearson, 1996). Also, a fine and/or a prison term could be imposed if a child uses a gun owned by the parent to commit a crime and/or a fine to imprison parents whose children fail to attend school or skip school more than 10 times in a year (Parsely, 1991). The following includes the types of parental legal responsibility for crimes committed by their children:

Damage and Restitution

Numerous states require parents to pay restitution for damages caused by their children. For example, in Hawaii and Utah, parents are responsible for the cost of damages caused by the graffiti of their children. In Florida, parents are responsible for the costs of their children's criminal prosecution. In Oregon, parents are responsible for any damages caused by their children. In New Jersey, parents must complete community service if their children violate a curfew law. In Oklahoma, parents must complete community service if their children possess an illegal firearm (Juvenile Justice Clearinghouse, 2006).

Tort Liability—Tort liability for damages caused by delinquent youth is yet another way States traditionally have held parents accountable for the misdeeds of their children (Geis & Binder, 1991). Hawaii, Florida, Louisiana, Massachusetts, and New Jersey do not place a limit on the amount of recovery. Today, all States except New Hampshire and New York have provisions holding parents civilly responsible for youth crime, with an average maximum recovery amount of $4,100 (Pearson, 1996).

Parental Involvement

While some States impose criminal liability on parents of delinquent youth, many more have enacted less stringent types of parental responsibility laws in the past 2 years. For example, some accountability initiatives require increased parental involvement in juvenile proceedings. Recent initiatives in Kansas, Michigan, and Texas require parents to attend the hearings of children adjudicated delinquent or face contempt charges. New legislation in Alabama, Kansas, Kentucky, and West Virginia amends existing laws to require parents to pay the court costs associated with these proceedings (Juvenile Justice Clearinghouse, 2006).

Initiatives to encourage parent and child togetherness are yet another approach incorporated into parental responsibility legislation in some States. In the past 2 years, Colorado, Florida, Louisiana, Missouri, and Texas have enacted legislation that requires parents and children to participate in community service activities after the youth has been in trouble with the law. In addition, new laws in Arizona, Florida, Indiana, Kansas, Kentucky, North Carolina, North Dakota, and Oregon require parents to attend counseling or other court-ordered treatment programs. Recent legislation in Arkansas, Colorado, Texas, and Wisconsin requires adult participation in parent training and responsibility courses. Often, involvement in these types of programs is a diversion option, with participation deferring any further punitive sanction from the court (Juvenile Justice Clearinghouse, 2006).

Enforcement of Parent Responsibility Laws

For the most part, parental responsibility laws have been met with mixed reviews. Some have researched such laws and have found they are rarely enforced on a consistent or frequent basis. The more important message sent by these laws is to shape the boundaries between acceptable and unacceptable parental behavior. With this in mind, these laws seem to shape a community's norms about parenting (Harris, 2006). For law enforcement, parental responsibility laws may need other avenues of resolution beyond an arrest. Again, it becomes clear that conflict resolution may have a place in the daily routine of law enforcement officers.

Legal Guidelines for Adolescence

There are legal guidelines for adolescents which should be stated in general terms for law enforcement officers entering the parental responsibility arena. In most jurisdictions, the age of majority for legal rights and responsibilities is age 18. This means things such as voting, buying tobacco products, entering the military, driving rules and privacy issues. In most States, the age of majority for alcohol consumption is age 21. Adolescents face criteria such as under the age of 16 being labeled as Juvenile Delinquents as it applies to criminal responsibility. In most States, age 16-19 is deemed Youthful Offender status which implies that if an adolescent is a first-time offender(for criminal offenses other than murder) and falls between the ages of 16 and 19, they are eligible for Youthful Offender status by the Court, which means that they are not convicted of a crime, their record is sealed and they are usually sentenced to probation and/or community service and restitution. The other criteria for parental responsibility in most jurisdictions regards financial responsibility by parents for the debts of their minor children (under age 21 in most States). This raises the issue of legal emancipation, which can be granted as young as age 16. The argument can still be made for not granting legal emancipation for issues such as marrying under the age of 18 and being financially independent from parents. The final area of involvement with adolescents by law enforcement may fall within the Education Law. Families and schools interact, in most jurisdictions, regarding the compulsory age of attendance rules, which are age 5-21 in most States. The rules regarding attendance may be called into question with law enforcement as it pertains to habitual truancy. School districts are mandated to have attendance policies which, if not adhered to, may result in the filing of PINS (person in need of supervision) petitions in Family Court. In most states, minors may voluntarily withdraw from school at either age 16 or 17. These rules are also affected by the employment status of the student.

Case Study

Mark and Jane had been dating for over a year and were now, at age 17, about to enter their senior year at their local high school, Jefferson High. Mark was the star soccer player on the varsity team and Jane was an honor student. They both planned on college following graduation. It was late August, with only a couple of weeks before the start of the school year, when Jane called Mark and was crying hysterically. "My mother and stepfather just threw me out of the house!" Jane screamed. "I don't know what to do – please pick me up at the end of my street in 10 minutes – we need to talk, Mark." Mark got into his car and immediately left to pick Jane up.

As he approached her street, he saw her running with a large travel bag over her arm and she appeared to be crying. He pulled up beside her and she got in his car.

"Thank you for rescuing me from my parents, Mark!" Mark reached over and held her as she sobbed uncontrollably and tried to tell him what happened. She regained her composure and began to explain that she had come home from work to find her parents waiting in the kitchen to speak to her. They began yelling at her and accusing her of spending too much time with Mark over the summer and neglecting her preparations for the coming school year. They told her that if she continued going out with Mark every night, disobeying her curfew and generally, not abiding by their rules, that she would not be going to college next year. They explained that she would lose her chance at a scholarship and forfeit her opportunities for success if she didn't break up with Mark immediately. Jane went on to tell Mark that they gave her an ultimatum—break up with him or leave their house. She chose to leave the house.

Jane was now in a panic. She didn't know what to do or where to go. Mark suggested that they go to his house and talk to his parents. Jane had always liked Mark's parents and had great respect for them. They had always treated her as a part of their family, including her in all holidays, birthdays and family vacations. Most of all, she trusted them.

They pulled into Mark's driveway and saw both cars in the driveway. They decided to go in and talk to his parents about Jane's situation. Jane left her travel bag and other belongings in the car and they went into the house. Mark's parents were in the kitchen preparing dinner when they walked in. "Hi, Jane, how are you?" Mark's mother asked. Jane began to cry again and both parents asked what was wrong. Mark suggested they all go into the living room to sit and discuss the matter. Jane composed herself and began to tell Mark's parents the story. They were shocked and saddened at the turn of events and asked Jane if there was anything they could do to help. Mark asked his parents if Jane could stay with them until her parents calmed down. Mark's parents said they would allow Jane to stay, but only if it were absolutely true that she couldn't go home. Jane thanked them and said she just needed some time to think about the whole situation and, hopefully, her parents would have a change of heart and call her to come home. Mark's parents suggested that Jane call her parents to tell them where she was and to let them know that she didn't intend to make this a permanent arrangement. Jane agreed and used her cell phone to call her parents. When she spoke to them, her mother was still very angry, she shouted into the phone that she didn't care where Jane was and that it was her choice to leave.

Jane unpacked her things in the upstairs guest room and came down to dinner with Mark and his parents and his younger sister, April. They had a very nice dinner together, and as Jane was helping to clean up, Mark's mother again said to her that she was welcome to stay with them on a temporary basis, but that the effort should be made to reconcile with her parents. Jane agreed. One week passed and no calls came from Jane's parents. The calls that Jane made to them were ignored and unanswered. When Jane would make contact with her mother, she would hang up the phone sobbing. Her mother appeared to be unwavering in her anger toward Jane. At the end of the second week, and as the school year was quickly approaching, Mark's parents asked to sit down and speak with both of them about Jane's situation. They all met in the family room and began to discuss the situation. Mark's mom began the discussion.

"Jane, you know that we are all very fond of you and would do anything to help you. You have been a helpful and pleasant guest to have in our home, but it's time to think about going home before school starts."

Jane began to cry and stated her fear and frustration over her parents' silence and inability to see her point of view. She didn't feel that the punishment they gave was deserved. She stated that she missed her family and wanted to go home, but not on their terms. At this point, Mark's dad suggested that they call the local police officer, Officer Briggs, whom they knew to have extensive experience with parent/child matters and mediation. They asked Jane and Mark if they would agree to mediation between Jane and her parents, facilitated by Officer Briggs. Jane said that she would be agreeable, and, in fact, she believed that her parents knew Officer Briggs and respected him. Mark's dad said that he would contact Officer Briggs and have him set up the session as soon as possible.

Mark's dad called Officer Briggs the next day and explained the situation to him. However, Jane's mother also had called that day and demanded a PINS petition be filed. Officer Briggs concluded that Jane's family would be torn apart by such an act and asked if she and her husband would agree to mediate. The meeting was set up for the next day at the police station, pending agreement from Jane's parents to come. They both agreed based on their trust of Officer Briggs. The next day came and Mark dropped Jane off at the police station for the mediation session. Jane went into the conference room and saw her mother at the table, but her stepfather wasn't there. She asked about him and her mother explained that it was really between her and Jane, and that he would abide by their agreement, if there was one. Officer Briggs came into the room, said hello, and asked Jane and her mother to sit down.

"Let me begin by thanking both of you for coming to this mediation session. I know both of you; however, I need to ask if you both feel comfortable with me acting as mediator. This means that you see me as a neutral who will not take sides, and that you trust me to handle this session? I need your agreement, one at a time, before I can go forward with the session."

Both parties said "yes" to the issue of neutrality.

"Next, I need to explain the mediation process and go over some ground rules with you. As I discuss each rule, I need you to both agree before we go forward. Mediation is a process of communication between the two of you where I will remain neutral, not judge, and not come to a decision for you on these matters. I don't know very much about your situation. Mark's dad called and told me that Jane has been living with them for a couple of weeks after a disagreement between the two of you. He did express his desire to have you reunite as family as soon as possible. He said that he and his family did not want to interfere; but rather, were there to help if you needed it. Do either one of you have any questions at this point?"

They said "no."

"Then let's proceed to the ground rules. The first rule is: No name calling, no foul language and no interrupting each other."

They both said, "Yes."

"The second ground rule involves equal time to speak and addressing each other directly. You do not need to speak to me. I will be listening and possibly taking notes, if you want written agreement, but I will not be part of your conversation. That is between the two of you as mother and daughter."

They both said "yes" to this ground rule.

"Finally, I must ask if either of you have any commitments that would cause you to get up and leave before the end of the session, which would be about an hour?"

They both said they could stay as long as needed.

"Good," Officer Briggs replied, "let's get started. Who wants to begin? And remember – one at a time."

Jane's mom offered to begin and Jane agreed. She began to explain how angry and frustrated she had been for many months involving Jane's behavior. She felt that Jane was spending too much time with Mark, and, by doing so, throwing away her chances at college and the continuing honor roll grades that she had been receiving. She said that she couldn't believe that Jane would betray her by moving into Mark's house and she wondered what kind of people Mark's parents were to allow such a thing. She explained that her rules were important to follow and, that she felt disrespected by Jane for her running away to Mark's house. She said that she was finished speaking for now and Officer Briggs thanked her and asked Jane to give her side of the story.

"Finally, I get to tell my side of this story," Jane replied. "Mom, you know that I didn't run away, you kicked me out! I had nowhere to go and fortunately, Mark and his family care enough about me to invite me into their home. I called you numerous times and you ignored my calls, hung up on me or screamed at me, what was I supposed to do, Mom?"

At this point Jane began to cry and so did her Mom. Officer Briggs offered the tissue box to them and said that they should take a moment to compose their thoughts – then resume the session. Jane's mom said that she felt a lot of pressure from her husband, Jane's stepfather, to set rules and discipline Jane more. She also expressed her fear of Jane losing what she had worked so hard to attain by spending too much time with Mark. She admitted that she shouldn't have been so harsh and that she loved Jane and missed having her at home.

At this point, Officer Briggs interrupted and began to recap what they had discussed so far.

"It sounds to me like you both were angry, lost your tempers, and have regrets about what happened between you a couple of weeks ago. Jane, you say that you want to lead your own life, which includes being with Mark and keeping your grades up for a college scholarship. Your mom has said that she only wants what's best for you, misses you and wants the family reunited. Is that fair to say for both of you?" Officer Briggs asked.

"Yes," they both replied.

"Ok, where do you want to go from here?" he asked. Jane and her mother reached their hands out to each other across the table and agreed that they wanted to settle the dispute.

"Good, let's proceed," said Officer Briggs. "At this point, we can draw up an agreement of rules to abide by for both of you, or you can have a verbal agreement."

They both replied that they would like a verbal agreement.

Officer Briggs said, "That is fine, what would you like to talk about?" Jane said that she would agree to come home if her step-father would agree to let her and her mother work out their differences. Her mother said that she would talk to him. Jane said that she would continue to work hard and not let her relationship with Mark interfere. She also agreed to her mother's request for a midnight curfew on weekends and only a couple of school nights out for school-sponsored activities and home by 10 pm on school nights. They both agreed that they could live with these agreements.

Officer Briggs expressed his hope that this mediation would clear the air between them and help resolve their differences. He also said that he would be available if they wanted to come back for future sessions, and, if Jane's stepfather decided that he wanted to participate.

"Thank you both for coming and good luck to you," Officer Briggs said. Jane and her Mom got up, hugged each other and thanked Officer Briggs for helping them.

Conflict Resolution and Parental Responsibility

Law enforcement officers may want to consider some form of conflict resolution when considering calls that surround parental responsibility, physical, mental and sexual abuse being the exception. Actually, many of the disputes between parents and children may suffer if some form of punitive action is enforced (Williams, 1998). For example, in the case study, Jane's mother wanted Officer Briggs to file a PINS petition against her daughter. The eventual reconciliation may have never taken place if such an order was filed. The many gray areas surrounding the law and parental responsibility leaves Officer Briggs to consider mediation as a remedy to their dispute.

Even in cases where laws are being broken, such as a student being truant from school beyond the legal number of days, are filled with variations, until the law enforcement officer has all of the facts. There may have been a death in the family and no one was informed. Or, as in the case study, someone has run away and has created a dispute that makes it difficult to return. In these cases, the perception a community has for the role of law enforcement may allow an officer to practice conflict resolution while still upholding the law (Cooper, 1999). The following are issues to consider when a law enforcement officer decides to resolve a dispute between a parent and a child.

- Do both sides have a legitimate point of view?

- Would giving both sides equal power to express their opinions help or hurt the dispute?

- Are both sides reacting out of anger when they ask for some form of legal action?

- Would mediating between parent and child run the risk of breaking any parental responsibility laws?

- Could mediation serve a higher benefit by helping the community as a whole?

- Are both parties capable of living by an agreement they have produced?

These and other issues can give law enforcement an opportunity to uphold the law, but also accomplish something for the common good. Police officers armed with mediation skills can handle these types of scenes substantively, avoid escalating the level of the dispute, and avert a repeat call-for-service. A police department trained in mediation and arbitration also maintains a better reputation with citizens and strengthens community policing philosophy, missions and programs (Cooper, 1999). Adolescence is a difficult time for both parents and law enforcement. Working together may help adolescent children find the common ground necessary for a peaceful community.

Parent/Child Mediation

The dispute resolution process that brings parents and their children together to resolve family disputes takes on many forms. Some of the topics of these sessions are:

- family rules
- discipline
- curfews
- expectations of both sides
- educational issues
- driving issues
- friends
- alcohol and substance use
- motivational issues
- clear communication lines so that both sides share their feelings.

It is important as a mediator to refrain from taking sides. It is easy for law enforcement personnel to side with the parent. This only serves to further polarize the young person involved in the dispute. They will assume that you will be taking the parent's side and be more trusting if you remain neutral (Lang & Taylor, 2000). It will be especially difficult to remain neutral and not apply the law to the family dispute if you side with the parents. It is also a good idea, if possible, to train other young people to mediate so that you can solicit their assistance as co-mediators to better balance the dynamics of the parent/child conflict. Law enforcement reaches out to young people in other matters, such as solving crime — why not do the same with mediation?

Exercises

Responding to the Case Study (How would Officer Briggs respond to this call from a *legal point of view?*)

Responding to the Case Study (How would Officer Briggs respond to this call from a *conflict resolution point of view?*)

In the case study, what other types of alternatives could Officer Briggs point out to Jane and her mother?

What other issues do you think were important in the case study?

Can you see any other times that conflict resolution could be used in Parental responsibility cases?

What do you think would be appropriate follow-up to Officer Briggs mediation with Jane and her mother?

What would be your next plan of action if conflict resolution did not work?

Should an arrest be considered in this case?

Part II

Mediation Training

Chapter 10

MEDIATION FOR LAW ENFORCEMENT (REVIEW)

Introduction

In the last nine chapters we have discussed mediation skills and other conflict resolution remedies. The final chapter will be a review of these skills and how to use these skills when deemed appropriate when making a call as a law enforcement officer. Hopefully, specific training can take place where each person reading this book can become knowledgeable and have the ability to practice mediation. The following are those skills that seem most important to learn:

The Five Stages of Mediation

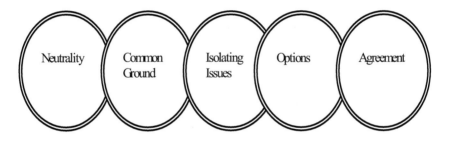

Neutrality | Common Ground | Isolating Issues | Options | Agreement

Creating Neutrality

The first step in creating a climate for mediation is to assure that equality and neutrality are intricately connected to the mediation process. A mediation climate may fail if equality and neutrality are not established from the beginning. In the case studies in the last nine chapters, we have seen law enforcement officers who decide to withhold judgment and practice some form of conflict resolution. In those chapters where mediation was used, the first step was to take a neutral stance regarding the dispute.

In all of these cases, the law enforcement officer should have ground rules for the parties to follow and both parties in dispute should have an opportunity to make an opening statement. These opening activities have a specific purpose in the mediation. They create a climate where the mediator is viewed as a neutral third party, and the opposing parties would be treated equally without imposing judgments or taking sides (Mayer, 2003).

Balance is another main concern facing a competent mediator. When one party speaks to the other, then the opposite party should have an opportunity to speak back. Creating a climate for mediation requires the mediator to remain neutral, so opposing parties have equal opportunities to express balanced points of view (Garcia, Vise & Whitaker, 2002). In successful mediations, equality, neutrality and balance must be upheld or people in dispute may not openly express their thoughts and feelings.

Neutrality Skills

Balancing Space—One of the most effective ways to accomplish spatial balance is by having a room with a rectangular table and at least three chairs. The mediator sits between the mediating parties and communicates the same verbal and non-verbal gestures to both of them. If the mediator makes a gesture to one, then a reciprocal gesture is made to the other. For example, if the law enforcement officer looks at one party while discussing ground rules, then it may be important to look equally at the other.

Balancing Time—is the ability of the mediator to listen equally to both parties in dispute. If one party talks for five minutes, then the other party should have an opportunity to talk for an equal amount of time. Balancing time between both people in dispute can be upheld with a ground rule requesting equal time when discussing mediation issues. This may be especially important in the beginning of mediation when rules are tested and behavior is established for discussions. If people balance their time in the beginning portion of mediation, then balance has more probability of following through the rest of the mediation process.

Balancing Judgments—is making sure that both parties have an opportunity to speak their minds, and are not judged by the mediator or by each other. Balancing the opening portion of mediation by not making judgments sends a message that the mediator's purpose is to facilitate communication, not judge right or wrong. Keeping this in mind, mediators should be careful not to make any verbal or non-verbal gestures that may be misinterpreted as a judgment, either positively or negatively.

Developing Ground Rules — Confusion and miscommunication are reduced if a mediator successfully describes certain ground rules to the parties before the mediation begins. Ground rules are the foundation of any mediation and remain the most important element in a climate of neutrality. The following are a typical set of ground rules in an informal mediation conducted by a law enforcement officer:

- There are times during mediation when emotions may run high but can we agree to treat each other with common courtesy?

- Sometimes in the heat of emotions we may call each other names that stop the mediation process. If this happens, can we agree to regroup and use different language when talking to each other?

- Can we agree to give each party an equal chance to discuss their point of view?

Making an Opening Statement — The conversation between disputing parties begins with an opening statement from both parties. The Law enforcement officer may say to the disputants, "Who would like to start?" After agreement over who will begin, the law enforcement officer may say to the first disputant, "Can you share your side of the dispute?" After the first disputant's opening statement is made, then the other disputant gives an opening statement or responds to the first disputant's statement. When both opening statements are completed, the law enforcement officer should encourage the disputants to engage in open discussion.

Finding Common Ground

Finding common ground seems an unnatural next step in the mediation process. Law enforcement officers are trained to solve problems by analyzing people's differences, but in mediation, looking for what people have in common becomes the next step. Finding common ground is probably the strongest tool a mediator possesses in guiding people to successful resolution of their disputes (Lang and Taylor, 2000). For example, in Chapter 9 Jane and her mother did not need a mediator who analyzed their communication problem and then demonstrated how to fix it. They required someone, other than themselves, to actually "shrink" the communication breakdown problem to a size that was workable and less overwhelming (Ladd, 1989). Officer Briggs pointed out common ground on such items as: both were angry, lost their tempers and had regrets about what they said. Agreements from Suzanne and Jane on all of these pieces of common ground, made their dispute reasonable and manageable. In effect, finding common ground changed how both of them perceived the problem. Without common ground, the problem seemed overwhelming and out of control but with common ground, both began to speak with each other. The mediator's responsibility after creating a climate of neutrality is to allow people an opportunity to vent their thoughts and feelings; while the mediator constantly looks for common ground (Ladd, 2005). The more established common ground, the less overwhelming are people's perceptions of the dispute, and the closer people come to solving their problems.

Common Ground Skills

Common ground can be at the heart of successful mediations. A mediator may enter mediation only to find disputants polarized against each other; where mediating an agreement may appear unlikely. Common ground brings disputing parties closer together and demonstrates that people in conflict are not that different from each other, and may have certain fundamental common beliefs. Some of these common beliefs are based on issues such as: both parties agreeing they were friends before the dispute began. Other beliefs are based on commonly held emotions such as: both parties agreeing they have been frustrated with each other for quite some time (Ladd, 2005).

Common Ground Surrounding Issues – During a mediation session both parties might say they agree to a particular issue discussed in the conversation. For example, during a mediation where harassment is involved, the officer may state that both sides seem to be harassing each other. If both parties agree, you have found issues-oriented common ground—focusing on the mutual harassment taking place.

Common Ground Surrounding Emotions—Sometimes, mediators help people in dispute, by showing how their conflict has emotionally affected both of them. When this happens, the mediator is pointing out emotions-oriented common ground. An example of this could be, "So you agree that the dispute has angered both of you and that you both are becoming frustrated and stuck." Again, if they both agree, you have found emotions-oriented common ground, focusing on anger leading to frustration.

The more common ground found in mediation, the less confusion over isolating issues in a dispute. Common ground limits conflict by creating agreement (Freeman, 1999). It gives people, in dispute, an opportunity to perceive important issues that still need discussion. It focuses people's thoughts and feelings while eliminating extraneous information from the mediation process.

Isolating Issues

Isolating issues in mediation can be a different process than found in other problem solving techniques, such as isolating issues in a court of law (Bennet & Herman, 1997). A court of law follows logical methods for problem solving but are less effective in mediation. The reason lies in their inability to let emotions surface in the mediation process. Mediations are a blend of issues and emotions and both may need consideration for mediations to be effective. The issues in a dispute can be only part of the story. Some disputes carry unforgettable emotional experiences that carry as much importance as the issues (Sautter, 1995). Also, isolating issues too early in the mediation process can be a common mistake made by mediators with superior problem solving skills but little awareness of people's emotions. People may need time to work through these emotional roadblocks affecting their lives before issues seem relevant. As a rule when people, in mediation, stop venting and start repeating their important issues, a law enforcement officer may realize that the main issues of those in dispute have reached the point of negotiation and need to be isolated.

Isolating Issues Skills

Isolating issues requires mediators to make mediations specific and clear. Here may be where having a clear understanding of the dispute, becomes a valuable asset. Two important skills needed by mediators when disputing parties are venting their feelings or telling their stories are paraphrasing and reframing—especially when a conversation is not working and intervention is needed to put the discussion back on track (Ladd, 2005):

Paraphrasing—is the ability of the mediator to stop mediation and briefly describe what is being said, up to that point in the mediation. Paraphrasing becomes useful when emotions run high or when communication bogs down. Paraphrasing people's conversations can put their discussions into perspective while allowing emotions to be expressed freely. These paraphrases can become important to the disputants in successful mediations. They can convey what has been accomplished and how far they must go before reaching an agreement.

Also paraphrasing is a technique for filling in those silent moments during mediation, when disputants have bogged down and have difficulty talking to each other. At these moments, a review of the themes previously mentioned gives the mediation a renewed focus that places the mediation back on track. Usually when a silent moment occurs, one or both disputing parties may turn to the mediator for direction. At moments like these, paraphrasing what has been accomplished may give new direction to the conversation.

Reframing—is another important skill that "softens the blow" when people shock each other with their inappropriate remarks during a mediation. This can happen when language becomes too harsh, the message too overpowering or when the other party cannot understand what is being said. When an inappropriate remark is delivered, the mediator reframes these remarks to the party who is having difficulty receiving the other's message (Bandler & Grinder, 1982). A mediator takes the unreceivable message of one party and puts it another way or reframes it until it is clearly received by the other party. For example, if one disputant says to another disputant in mediation regarding an Order of Protection as found in Chapter 2, "You have been a liar and a cheat when you said you would pay me the money. You lied to me!" When reframed by a mediator, it may sound something like this, "What John is trying to say is that you agreed to pay the money, but you haven't done that yet." Reframing avoids potential breakdowns in people's discussions and makes what is said to others more acceptable, allowing both parties to continue in the mediation process.

Choosing Options

Choosing options can be the creative "empowerment" stage in mediation. People are encouraged, at this point, to develop options for resolving their disputes. For the most part, mediators keep their role to a minimum in this stage of the mediation process; whatever is negotiated will affect the disputing parties, not the mediator. However, having people empowered to negotiate options is what mediation is all about. Mediators set the stage for negotiations by creating a climate of neutrality, finding common ground and isolating issues. It is now the role of the parties, in dispute, to seek viable options to these problems (Ladd, 2005). Mediators help in the negotiation in a minor way by reminding people of previously isolated issues, pointing out any new issues that may need discussion and presenting one party's option to the other party in an understandable, reasonable manner. At this stage in the mediation process, mediators act as referees in the bargaining taking place between people in dispute. They do not suggest what options either person should choose nor do they give advice on what options are best suited for their needs.

Also, certain mediating parties, taking part in negotiations, may need the help of the mediator; especially when the participating parties in dispute are having difficulty getting started in the negotiation process. The mediator may remind them of isolated issues or give them general categories for consideration, but does not direct them in negotiating any specific item in any specific way.

Sometimes, staying out of the negotiations becomes difficult for mediators especially in law enforcement where officers have competently held positions of authority and where giving direction may be a large part of their jobs. However, mediation is a democratic process based on free choice and it adheres to the principle that people have the ability to solve their problems. Creating a climate of neutrality, finding common ground and isolating issues are activities that allow people to find acceptable answers to their disputes.

Effective mediators know that timing remains a more effective skill in the negotiation stage of mediation than over-involvement. Knowing when to remind people of issues or when to move on to the next round of negotiations on a new issue becomes the responsibility of the mediator (Hammond, 2003).

Choosing Options Skills

The negotiation stage in mediation empowers people to develop options that reflect their thoughts and feelings in the mediation process. During this stage of mediation, democratic principles are given an opportunity to be employed through negotiation. The following are three common types of options found in everyday mediations:

Options Based on Consensus — One form of option people in dispute consider are options based on consensus. Common sense tells us why consensus-based options are popular in mediation. These options are more likely to succeed, because they benefit both parties in dispute. Options that are mutually beneficial to both parties also add to the mediation's common ground. This style of options creates consensus, much in the manner that finding common ground helps in isolating issues (Fisher & Ury, 1991). For example, a petit larceny charge involving shoplifting, may give the store owner and the shoplifter an opportunity to reach consensus on what type of action is fair and reasonable so the shoplifting does not happen again.

Point/Counter Point Options — Another type of option found in mediations is concerned with balancing one option against another. Point/Counter Point options are the "Quid Pro Quo" formula in negotiating options in mediation (Williams, 1998). For example, in a trespass call involving a barking dog complaint, the dog's owner agrees to keep the dog inside at night if the other party agrees to stop gossiping to the neighbors. However, balance is the key word in point/counterpoint options. If one party is willing to do ten things for the other but the other has agreed to do nothing in return, then the negotiation becomes out-of-balance and probably will fail.

Caucusing — is a technique for meeting individually with one party for negotiation purposes while the other party remains outside the mediation room. Caucusing may be useful when hidden agendas are breaking down negotiations and begin to stonewall effective options. By having the other party wait outside, the mediator is able to talk candidly and avoid awkward moments for both parties (Susskind & McKearney, 1999). However, caucusing seems a method of last resort and not as a general practice in creating options in mediation. Overuse of caucusing may limit shared participation needed for both parties in creating mutually acceptable agreements. One method for avoiding overuse of caucusing can be to find a substantial amount of mutually agreed-on common ground. The more common ground, the more people are willing to face each other and negotiate viable options for successful agreements (Ladd, 2005).

Making an Agreement

After options are negotiated, mediators encourage disputants to make an agreement that is fair and reasonable. Reaching agreement is the responsibility of the people in dispute; however, formatting the agreement is the responsibility of the mediator (Folberg & Taylor, 1984). In the final step of a successful mediation, the mediator helps in the development of a plan based on the wishes of both people in dispute. How words were phrased and the type of language used, is considered in personalizing their mediation agreement. If the language is confusing either party or the mediator finds discrepancies that were overlooked, then the rough draft of the agreement would be rephrased until agreeable to everyone. Finally, agreements can be written or verbal, depending on the officer and the parties agreeing. More formal mediations are usually written because details hold considerable weight in final agreements. Less formal mediations do not need a written agreement and may sustain an informal process, possibly concluding with a review of the agreed issues and a "hand shake." Either way, mediation is successful when both parties agree to the plan either verbally or in writing.

Agreements Skills

A mediator's responsibility is to draw up agreements that do not judge either party in dispute. By describing options acceptable to both parties for inclusion into the final agreement, mediators create a descriptive framework that is free of generalizations or judgments.

The Importance of Being Specific — The more specific the language, the higher probability people will honor their agreements. If the language in the agreement does not specifically describe, step by step, each point, then the agreement may lose its ability to give specific direction to those in dispute (Moore, 2003). Being specific also helps mediators avoid writing an agreement that is judgmental. Judgments are more concerned with themes, such as guilty vs. not guilty. Mediated agreements are not looking for winners and losers. They should be written so both parties specifically understand what they believe is an acceptable agreement.

Roadblocks to Successful Agreements:

Incomplete Agreements — One of the major roadblocks in reaching a successful agreement is when mediators fail to include isolated issues emerging earlier in the mediation. All isolated issues should be negotiated and options developed before reaching a final agreement. If this does not happen, agreements are viewed as incomplete and lose legitimacy in resolution of the dispute. It is important that mediators make sure isolated issues are represented in the final agreement in some form, either written or verbal.

Contingency Agreements — Another difficult roadblock to successful mediations is when an agreement is contingent on additional information or future performance by one or more parties in the dispute. Mediation runs into difficulties when one or both parties back out of the agreement by using excuses that additional information was not provided or agreeing only after observing if someone's behavior changes in the future. For example, a person in dispute may say, at a future date, "Additional information has changed my mind." Or, "Your behavior has changed my mind."

Agreements in Principle — When both parties agree in principle, but the details are not worked through, the agreement is weakened because the only agreement made is the intent to agree. Such agreements are usually vague and give little information for any specific behavioral or emotional changes. Agreements in principle are sometimes not legitimate agreements but a method for avoiding change. This happens especially when agreements are unbalanced and seem to favor one side. In this case, a person will agree in principle to end the mediation but with no intentions of living up to the agreement (Ladd, 2005).

Using the Language of the Disputants — Not all mediated agreements are written in the language of the disputants. An example of this can be found in custody and visitation mediations where the court requires a specific language to be included in the final documents. However, it is important for mediators within the limits placed on them, to come as close to the language discussed during the mediation process. It is most important that the mediated agreement reflect the words used during the options stage of the mediation. Agreements are stronger when disputants recognize their points of view being acknowledged, both in their negotiations and in the final agreement.

Keeping the Agreement Balanced — Balance is an issue resonating all through mediation and balance also should be reflected in the final agreement. Agreements that favor one party over the other either reflect a mediation that was out of balance from the beginning or became weighted to favor one party during final negotiations. Agreements that favor one side over another rarely work. Balance is a term that should be in the mediator's mind all through the mediation, and especially in drawing up the final agreement. In mediation, balance reflects fairness, and creating a fair and balanced process is one of mediation's major goals.

A Mediation Exercise

The following is a mediation checklist for evaluating your performance after completing mediation. Check off activities that took place and discuss with others, high points in the mediation and potential changes for making the next mediation more successful (Ladd, 2005).

Mediation Checklist

Creating Neutrality:
  Did I present the ground rules in an effective manner?
  Did I keep balance both temporally and spatially?
  Did I allow an ample opportunity for opening statements?
  Did I remain in control during this stage of mediation?
  Did I receive agreement on all ground rules before continuing?

Finding Common Ground:
  Did I find issues that both parties had in common?
  Did I successfully review common ground?
  Did I look for factual and emotional common ground?
  Did the common ground make the dispute more reasonable?
  Did mediating parties have an opportunity to vent their
      feelings?

Isolating Issues:
  Did the parties discuss issues when the venting slowed down?
  Did the parties repeat important issues over and over again?
  Did I remind people what issues were still in dispute?
  Did I reframe issues that were emotionally charged?
  Did I isolate issues for both parties in dispute?

Choosing Options:
  Did I empower mediating parties to solve their dispute?
  Were consensus and point/counterpoint options discussed?
  Did I suggest categories for discussion during negotiations?
  Did I paraphrase people's offers, making them more negotiable?
  Did I review the options accepted by both parties?

Making an Agreement:
  Did I write the agreement in the mediating parties' own words?
  Was the agreement balanced between both parties?
  Did I avoid contingency agreements?
  Did I make the agreement specific?
  Did I review the mediation agreement and thank both parties?

Mediation Short Notes

Creating Neutrality:

- The mediator is responsible for ground rules that will help disputants discuss their problems.

- The mediator must keep the mediation balanced both temporally and spatially.

- The mediator allows the disputants the opportunity for an opening statement.

- The mediator keeps power during this stage, in order to establish the climate.

- The mediator establishes agreement on all ground rules before continuing.

Finding Common Ground:

- The mediator looks for those themes that both parties have in common.

- The mediator reviews the common ground to show progress in the mediation.

- The mediator looks for factual and emotional common ground.

- By finding common ground, the dispute becomes more manageable.

- The disputants have an opportunity to vent during this stage.

Isolating Issues:

- The disputants are ready for issues when the venting slows down.

- Disputants will repeat issues continuously when the issues are important.

- The mediator's role is to let disputants know the issues still in dispute.

- Mediators reframe issues that are still emotionally charged.

- The issues must be developed on both sides.

Choosing Options:

- It is important for disputants to negotiate their issues during this stage.

- Disputants can create options by consensus or point/ counterpoint procedures.

- The mediator does not suggest options but may suggest categories to cover. Mediator sometimes paraphrases offers to the other disputant.

- The mediator reviews the progress being made in negotiations.

Making an Agreement:

- Agreements are fair when they are balanced between both parties.

- Agreements are fair when they reflect the options in the disputants' words.

- Contingency agreements are power plays not true agreements.

- More specific agreements have a higher chance for success.

- The agreement stage can be a productive time to review the mediation.

BIBLIOGRAPHY

Anderson, T. (2002) Protests and the politics of protection: In dealing with protesters, companies must uphold the civil rights of the activist while simultaneously protecting property and personnel. Security Management, Vol. 46 (4) pp. 53+.

Applebaum, A. W. & Klemmer, H. (1984) Shoplifting. Menninger Perspective (Fall) 16-19.

Arias, M. L. (2007) Vandalism and legal issues to address. Irvine, CA: Internet Business Law Services.

Axelsen, K. L. (1995) Problems with punitive damages for political protest and civil disobedience. Environmental law, 25 (2) pp. 495-511.

Bandler, R., & Grinder, J. (1982) Reframing: Neuro-linguistic programming and the transformation of meaning. Moab, UT: Real People.

Barnes, E. B. (2006) Culture, conflict and mediation in the Asian Pacific. Lanham, MD: University Press of America.

Barsky, A. (2000) Conflict resolution for the helping professions. Stamford, CT: Brooks/Cole.

Bazemore, S. Gordon and Schiff, Mara, eds. (2001). Restorative Community Justice : Repairing Harm and Transforming Communities. Anderson Pub. Co.

Beers J. (1997) The Mediator's Handbook. New York: Friends Conflict Resolution Programs.

Bennett, M., Herman, M. (1997) The art of mediation. New York: NITA

Bergen, R. K. (1998) Issues in intimate violence. Thousand Oaks, CA: Sage Publications.

Blanchfield, K. & Ladd, P. (1989) "Appropriate Dispute Resolution: Methods for Different Types of Disputes" Expanding Horizons: Theory and Research in Dispute Resolution, Washington D.C.: American Bar Association Press, August 1989.

Blanchfield, T. & Lenahan, T. (2004) New York Security Officer Training Manual. Binghamton, NY: Gould Publications.

Blanchfield K. and Ladd P. (1989) "Appropriate Dispute Resolution: Methods for Different Types of Disputes" Expanding

Blakely, E. H. & Gibbs, P. (2000) Gatekeeping the bsw programs. New York: Columbia University Press. Horizons: Theory and Research in Dispute Resolution, Washington, DC: American Bar Association Press.

Blau, T. (1994) Families apart. New York: Putnam Pub.

Bloomer, S.T., Ruedt, D. E. & Sipe, T. A. (2002) Child support Payment and child visitation perspectives from nonresident fathers and resident mothers. Journal of Sociology & Social Welfare, 29 (2), 77+.

Brinkman, R. & Kirchner, R., (1994) Dealing with people you can't stand: How to bring out the best of people at their worst. Toronto: McGraw Hill.

Brinson, J. A., Fisher, T. A. & Kottler, J.A. (2004) Cross cultural conflict resolution strategies for counselors. Journal of Counseling Development, Vol. 82 (3) PP.294+.

Bureau of Justice Statistics and Crime Data Brief (2003) Intimate Partner Violence 1993-2000. Washington D.C.

Bush, H. & Folger, R. (1994) The promise of mediation. San Francisco: Jossey-Bass Pub.

Center for the Advancement of Women (2003) Progress and perils: New agenda for women. Center for the Advancement of Women, June 2003.

Chamberlain, P., Eddy, M., & Whaley, R. B. (2004) The prevention of violent behavior by chronic and serious male juvenile offenders: A 2-year followup of a randomized clinical trial. Journal of Emotional and Behavioral Disorders,12 (1), 2.

Claiborne, L. (2005) Investigate the levels of dating abuse among American teenagers. Liz Claiborne Inc., Feb. 2005.

Coates, Robert, Kalanj, Boris & Umbreit, Mark (1994) Victim Meets Offender: The Impact of Restorative Justice and Mediation. Criminal Justice Press.

Cohen, D. & Vandello, J. (1998) Meanings of Violence. Journal of Legal Studies, 27 (44), 567-569.

Connelly, J., G. Smith (2002) Politics of environment: From theory to practice, New York: Routledge.

Cooper, C. (1999) Mediation and arbitration for law enforcement officers. Lanham, MD: University Press of America.

Cutting, R. H. (2001) "One man's ceilin' is another man's floor": Property rights as the double-edged sword. Environmental Law, Vol. 31 (4) pp. 894+.

Dachman, K. A. & Leving, J. M. (1997) Father's rights: Hard hitting & fair advice for every father involved in a custody dispute. New York: Basic Books.

Damon, J. E. (1988) Shopaholics: Serious help for addicted spenders. Los Angeles: Price Stern Sloan.

Davidson, H. (1996) No Consequences -- Re-examining Parental Responsibility Laws, 7 Stan. L & Pol'y Rev. 23, 25 (1996) (citing P. Thomas Mason, Child Abuse and Neglect, Part I: Historical Overview, Legal Matrix and Social Perspective, 50 N.C.L. Rev. 293302 (1972)).

Dutton, D. G. (1995) The batterer. New York, NY: Basic Books.

Fagan, J. (1996) The criminalization of domestic violence: Promises and limits. NIJ Research Report, pp. 58.

Family Court Act, Section 530.12 (2004) Flushing: Looseleaf Law.

Federal Government (1968) The Uniform Custody Jurisdiction Act.

Friedman, D. (1995) Towards a structure of indifference: The social origins of maternal custody. New York: Aldine de Gruyter Pub.

Fisher, R., Ury, D. (1991) Getting to yes: Negotiating agreement without giving in. In Bruce Patton 2nd Ed. New York: Penguin Books.

Folberg, J., Taylor, A. (1984) Mediation: A comprehensive guide to resolving conflicts without litigation. San Francisco: Jossey-Bass.

Freeman, L. (1999) Common ground: Letters to a world community of Mediators. New York: Continuum International Publishing Group.

Garcia, A. C., Vise, K., Whitaker, S. P. (2002) Disputing neutrality: A case of a bias complaint during mediation. Conflict Resolution Quarterly. 20 (2) 205-230.

Garrity J. & Baris G. H. (1994) Caught in the middle. Toronto: Lexington Books.

Gaylin, W. (2003) Hatred: The psychological descent into violence. New York: Public Affairs

Geis, G. & Binder, A. (1991) Sins of Their Children: Parental Responsibility for Juvenile Delinquency, 5 Notre Dame J.L. Ethics & Pub. Pol'y 307.

Gladding, S (2002) Family Therapy: History, Theory and Practice. Upper Saddle River, NJ: Prentice Hall

Goodman, A. H. (1996) Basic skills for the new mediator. Rockville, Maryland: Soloman Publications.

Gottfredson, M. & Hirschi (1990) A genera of crime. Stanford: Stanford University Press.

Hankins, G., Hankins, C. (1998) Prescription for anger: Coping with angry feelings and angry people. New York: Warner Books.

Harris, L. J. (2006). An Empirical Study of Parental Responsibility Laws: Sending Messages, but What Kind and to Whom? Utah Law Review 2006 (2006): 5-34.

Harrison R. S. (2002) Community-based mediation programs: A case study and comparison. International Journal of Public Administration, Vol. 25 (11) 1427+.

Hefferman, W. C. (2001) Fourth amendment privacy interests. Journal of Criminal Law and Criminology, p. 1+.

Holtz-Munroe, A., Stuart, G. L., and Hutchinson, G. (1997) Violent versus nonviolent husbands: Differences in attachment patterns, dependency, and jealousy. Journal of Family Psychology. 11(3), 314-342.

Homant, R. J., Kelly, T. M. & Kennedy, D. B. (2003) Evaluation of an individualized treatment program for adolescent shoplifters. Adolescence, 38 (152), 725+.

Johnson, K.D. (2005) Vandalism break in guide no. 35. Washington, D.C.: Center for Problem Oriented Policing.

Juvenile Justice Clearinghouse (2006) Rockville, Maryland.

Konstan, V., Chernoff, M., Deveney, S. (2001) Toward forgiveness: The role of shame, guilt, anger, and empathy. Counseling and Values Volume 46, pp.26-37

Kuttner, R. (1999) The age of trespass. The American Prospect, Jan. 1999, p.6.

Ladd, P. (1989) Appropriate dispute resolution: Methods for different types of disputes. Expanding Horizons: Theory and Research in Dispute Resolution. Washington, D.C.: American Bar Association Press.

Ladd, P. (2005) Mediation, Conciliation and Emotions: A practitioner's Guide to Understanding Emotions in Dispute Resolution, Lanham, MD: University Press of America.

Lanceley, F. J., (2002) On scene guide for crisis negotiators. New York: CR Press.

Lane, E. (2003) Due process and problem-solving courts. Fordham Urban Law Journal, 30, (3) 955+.

Lang, M. D., Taylor, A. (2000) The making of a mediator. San Francisco, CA: Jossey-Bass.

Li, M.Q. & Merry, S. E. (1987) Cultural aspects of disputing. Honolulu, HI; Conflict resolution Series.

Lienman, M. & Mandell, R. (1996) Mediating custody and visitation. New York State Dispute Resolution Association, Albany, New York.

Looseleaf Law (2006) Penal and Criminal Procedure Law of the State of New York. Flushing, New York: Looseleaf Law Publications

Looseleaf Law (2004) Article 145 - Criminal Mischief and Related Offenses. Penal and Criminal Law of the State Of New York. Flushing, NY: Looseleaf Law Publications.

Mariani, C. & Sokolich, P. (1996) Domestic violence survival guide. Flushing, NY: Looseleaf Law Publications.

Marts, A. C. (1996) The generosity of Americans: Its source – Its achievements. New Jersey: Prentice Hall.

Mason, M. A. (2000) The custody wars: Why children are losing the legal battle and what we can do about it. New York: Basic Books.

Mayer, B. (2003) The dynamics of conflict resolution: A practitioner's guide. San Francisco: Jossey-Bass.

McCoey, C. E. (1990) The authoritative manual on the security issues in premises liability litigation. New York: Aegis Books.

Miller, J. G. (1997) African-American males in the criminal justice system. Phi Delta Kappa, 78 (10), 1.

Miller, T., Cohen, M. & Wiersema, B. (1996) Victim costs and consequences: A new look. National Institute of Justice Washington, D.C.: U. S. Department of Justice.

Mills, L. G. (1999b). A penchant for prejudice: Unraveling bias in judicial decision-making. Ann Arbor: University of Michigan Press.

Mitchell, J. H. (1998) Trespassing: An inquiry into the private ownership of land. Reading, MA: Perseus Pub.

Moore, D. B. (2003) The mediation process: Practical strategies for resolving conflict. San Francisco: Jossey-Bass.

Moore, D. B. (1996) Shame: Human universal or cultural con-
    struct? In, Shame and the Modern Self. edited by R. Dalzeill,
    D. Parker and I. Wright. Melbourne: Australian Scholarly
    Publishers.
Mosten, F.J. (1997) The Complete Guide to Mediation. Chicago:
    American Bar Association.
New Jersey Domestic Violence Guidelines (2006) N.J.S.A.
    2C:25-19. Domestic Violence Act, Trenton: New Jersey
    Supreme Court.
New Jersey Domestic Violence Guidelines (2006) N.J.S.A.
    2C:25-21cb. Domestic Violence Act, Trenton: New Jersey
    Supreme Court.
New Jersey Domestic Violence Act (2006) N.J.S.A. 2C:25-28.
    Domestic Violence Act, Trenton: New Jersey Supreme Court.
New York State Penal Law, Section 155.05 (2004) Penal Law and
    Criminal Procedure Law of the State of New York. Flushing,
    NY: Looseleaf Law Publications Inc.
New York State Penal Law, Section 120.13 (2004) Penal Law and
    Criminal Procedure Law of the State of New York. Flushing,
    NY: Looseleaf Law Publications Inc.
New York State Penal Law, Section 120.14 (2004) Penal Law and
    Criminal Procedure Law of the State of New York. Flushing,
    NY: Looseleaf Law Publications Inc.
New York State Penal Law, Section 120.15 (2004) Penal Law and
    Criminal Procedure Law of the State of New York. Flushing,
    NY: Looseleaf Law Publications Inc.
New York State Penal Law, Section 120.10 (2004) Penal Law and
    Criminal Procedure Law of the State of New York. Flushing,
    NY: Looseleaf Law Publications Inc.
New York State Penal Law, Title N, Section 240. (2005) New York
    State Penal Law and Criminal Procedure. Orlando, FL:
    LexisNexis Gould Publications.
New York State Penal Law, Title N, Section 240.20 (2005) New
    York State Penal Law and Criminal Procedure. Orlando, FL:
    LexisNexis Gould Publications.
New York State Penal Law, Section 240.25. (2005) New York Penal
    Law and Criminal Procedure. Orlando, FL: LexisNexis Gould
    Publications.

New York State Penal Law, Section 240.26. (2005) New York State Law Enforcement Handbook. Orlando, FL: LexisNexis Gould Publications.

New York State Penal Law, Section 240.30. (2005) New York State Criminal Law Handbook. Orlando, FL: LexisNexis Gould Publications.

Oberlander, L. B. (1995) Ethical responsibilities in child custody evaluations: Implications for evaluation methodology. Ethics & Behavior, 5 (4), 311.

Ohlin, J. B. & Stauber, A. (2003) The applicability of citizen's arrest powers to the hospitality industry. Journal of Hospitality & Tourism Research, San Francisco: Sage Publishing.

Parsley, Kathryn. Constitutional Limitations on State Power to Hold Parents Criminally Liable for the Delinquent Acts of Their Children, 44 Vand. L. Rev. 446, 453 (1991).

Pappalardo, W. J. (2002) Proofing schools against vandalism. School Administrator, Vol. 59 (6) pp. 32

Pearson, E. (1996) Parental Responsibility Laws: An Overview 62 (Aug. 6, 1996) (unpublished M. Public Affairs thesis, University of Colorado) (on file with author).

Pilluta, M. M., and J. K. Murnighan. (1996) Unfairness, anger, and spite: Emotional rejections of ultimatum offers. Organizational Behavior and Human Decision Processes. 68, 208-24.

Sanders, B. (2005) Youth crimes and youth culture in the inner city. New York: Routledge, pp.iii

Retzinger, S., Scheff. T. (1996) Strategies for community conferences: Emotions and social bonds. In Restorative Justice: International Perspectives. Edited by B. Galaway, and J. Hudson, 315-336. Monsey, NY: Criminal Justice Press.

Retzinger, S., & Scheff. T. (2001) Emotion, alienation, and narratives: Resolving intractable conflict. Mediation Quarterly. 18(12), 45-67.

Rosen, M. B. (2004) You bagged the shoplifter, now what? A policy of catching shoplifters and pushing for prosecutions may not be the best use of company resources. Security Management, 48 (4), 59+.

Ross, N. A. (1997) You be the judge: The complete Canadian guide to resolving legal disputes out of court. Toronto: John Wiley.

Rourke, F. (1955) Shoplifting: Its symbolic motivation. Journal of Social Therapy, 1: 95-99.

Sanders, B. (2005) Youth crimes and youth culture in the inner city. New York: Routledge, pp.iii

Sapsonek, D. T. (1983) Mediating child custody disputes. San Francisco: Jossey-Bass Pub.

Sautter, R. C. (1995) Standing up to violence. Phi Delta Kappa. 76 (5), 1-8.

Scharmess, G. (1996) Graffiti! Cities are fighting this message of decay. Planning Vol. 62 (12) PP. 13.

Scheff, T. J. (1994) Bloody revenge: Emotions, nationalism, and war. Boulder, CO: West view Press.

Sickmund, J. (2000). An analysis of juvenile court referrals: The prominence of retail fraud. Paper presented at the Annual Conference of Juvenile Court Judges, Reno, Nevada. Silverman, J. G., Raj, A. & Clements, K. (2004) Dating violence against adolescent girls and associated substance use, unhealthy weight control, sexual risk behavior, pregnancy and suicidality. Pediatrics, August, 2004.

Slade. D. C. (2000) Grandparents' rights. World and I, 15 (9), 12.

Slaikue, K. A., Pearson, J., Laced, J., Myers, F. C. (1985) Process and outcome in divorce mediation. Mediation Quarterly. 19, 55-74.

Smedes, L. (1985) Forgive and forget: Healing the hurts we don't deserve. San Francisco: Harper Collins

Snyder, H. (2000) Juvenile arrests 1999. Juvenile Justice Bulletin, U. S. Department of Justice, Office of Juvenile and Delinquency Prevention.

Stahl, A. L. (2006) Adolescence and vandalism. Washington, D.C.: Office of Justice and Delinquency Prevention

Stomfay-Stiz, A. M. (1994) Conflict resolution and peer mediation: Pathways to safer schools. Childhood Education, Vol. 70 (5) pp. 279+.

Susskind, L. E., McKearney, S. & Thomas-Larmer, J. (Eds.) (1999) The Consensus building handbook: A comprehensive guide to reaching an agreement. Thousand Oaks, CA: Sage.

Texas Penal Code (2006) Penal Code of the State of Texas (Section 9.42).

Thackrah, J. R. (2004) Dictionary of Terrorism. New York: Routledge

Theisen, C. (2004) The parent coach plan. Copyright 2004: All Rights Reserved.

Umbreit, M. (1997) Victim-offender Mediation in Criminal Conflict: Toward Restorative Justice. In E. Kruk (Ed.) Mediation and Conflict Resolution in Social Work and the Human Services. Chicago: Nelson-Hall.

Umbreit, Mark S., Vos, Betty, Coates, Robert B. and Brown, Katherine A. (2004) Facing Violence: The Path of Restorative Justice and Dialogue. Monsey, NY: Criminal Justice Press.

Virginia Code Commission (2004) Section 18.2-95 to 18.2-96. Code of Virginia 1950: 2004 Cumulative Supplement Annotated, Vol. 1 of 2, Publisher: Mathew Bender.

Volkan, V. (1998) Psychoanalytic perspective on intergroup hatred. Journal for Psychoanalysis of Culture and Society. 3 (1) 78-80.

Ward, C. (1974) The child in the city. New York: Van Nostrand Reinhold.

Weinberg, N. (1995) Does apologizing help? The role of self-blame and making amends in recovery and bereavement. Health and Social Work, 20 (4), 294+.

Werdegar, M. M. (1999) Enjoining the constitution: The use of public nuisance abatement injunctions against urban street gangs. Stanford Law Review 51, (2), 409.

West Encyclopedia (2005) Different definitions of vandalism. Stamford, CT: Thomas Gale Publishers

Whittingham M. D. (1981) The urge to destroy. Canadian Journal of Criminology, Vol. 23

Williams, M. (1998) Mediation: Why people fight and how to help them stop. Dublin, Ireland: -Poolbeg Press.

Winslade, J., Monk, G. (2000) Narrative mediation: A new approach to conflict resolution. San Francisco: Jossey-Bass.

Yau-Fai Ho, D., Fu, W. and Ng, S. M. (2004) Guilt, shame and embarrassment: Revelations of face and self. Culture and Psychology. 10 (1), 64-85.

Yee, A. (1999) Parental Responsibility in Juvenile Justice. January 1999, NCSL Legisbrief, Vol. 7 (3).

INDEX